Insight Series No. 1

Them and Us?

Frederick W. Boal is Professor of Human Geography at the Queen's University of Belfast. He has carried out research on ethnically divided societies over many years. He is the author of *Shaping a City* and co-editor of *Integration and Division: Geographical Perspectives on the Northern Ireland Problem*.

Margaret C. Keane is Head of Geography at St. Mary's College, Belfast, where she is also Director of the Centre for Research and Curriculum Development. Her research has centred on community division in Belfast.

David N. Livingstone is Professor of Geography at the Queen's University of Belfast. His most recent book is *The Geographical Tradition* and he is currently working on cultural and religious connections between Ulster and America in the nineteenth century.

Insight Series No. 1

Them and Us?

*Attitudinal Variation
Among Churchgoers in Belfast*

Frederick W. Boal
Margaret C. Keane
David N. Livingstone

The Institute of Irish Studies
The Queen's University of Belfast

1997

Published 1997
The Institute of Irish Studies
The Queen's University of Belfast
Belfast

© The authors

All rights reserved. No part of this publication may be reproduced, stored in a retrieval system, or transmitted in any form or by any means, electronic, photocopying, recording, or otherwise, without the prior permission of the publisher.

British Cataloguing-in-Publication Data. A catalogue record for this book is available from the British Library.

ISBN 0 85389 679 8

Printed by Textflow Services Ltd, Belfast
Cover designed by Rodney Miller Associates

Contents

Preface vii

I Introduction 1
II Catholic Churchgoers 7
III Protestant Churchgoers 68
IV 'Them and Us': Sameness and Difference 143
V Afterword 171

Appendices 173
Bibliography 231
Index 235

Preface

It is now commonplace to portray life in Northern Ireland in terms of two traditions, two communities, two religions, two cultures, two nations. For some considerable time, we have been concerned at this rhetoric and in particular at its inability to encompass the realities of life in the Province. An earlier investigation of attitudinal variation among Protestant churchgoers in the Belfast area had already alerted us to the inadequacy of an assumed uniformity stretching right across what is often referred to as 'the Protestant people.' This present study widens the dimensions of that endeavour by investigating the opinions of both Protestants *and* Catholics on a wide variety of social, political, and religious issues. The aim is thus to display something of the cultural variety that exists in contemporary Northern Irish society, a variety too often subsumed under all-too-convenient bi-polar labels. None of this, of course, is intended to deny the real and deep differences that do exist between Catholics and Protestants here, not least on matters to do with the constitutional future of Northern Ireland; but it is to insist that such stereotyping fails to take with sufficient seriousness the internal varieties within each of these groups and to hide—even suppress—genuine continuities both between and across them. This book, therefore, seeks to convey something of the cultural heterogeneity that too rarely surfaces in commentary on life in Northern Ireland.

In conducting a research project of these dimensions we have incurred a wide range of debts. In particular, the whole exercise could not have been been undertaken without financial backing from the European Regional Development Fund and the Central Community Relations Unit of the Northern Ireland Office, and we are therefore very pleased to acknowledge their support. At the Queen's University, Paul Compton and Brian Whalley, successive Directors of the School of Geosciences, facilitated various aspects of this research as did Martin O'Callaghan, Principal of St. Mary's College.

We owe a immense debt of gratitude to our two research associates on the project, Jahnet Gardiner and Rebecca Daniel, without whose indefatigable efforts this work could never have been completed. In a very real sense this book is the product of a team effort, and joining as members of such a team has been an enriching experience. The appointment of a Religious Advisory Panel proved to be a wise strategy and we are grateful to the following for their participation: Aidan Burns, Pauline Coll, John Dunlop, Tom Gardiner, Tom Kirk, Pamela Lockie, Ambrose Macauley, Christina O'Neill, Ian Paisley, Patrick Roche, David Stevens and Edgar Turner. Assistance of various kinds was provided by a number of other people, and we record particular thanks to Sandra Baillie, Kathy Boal and Maura Pringle. Students of the Queen's University and St. Mary's College assisted us with coding of questionnaire responses. Margaret McNulty and Brian Walker, at the Institute of Irish Studies, provided welcome encouragement to turn our findings into a book.

Most of all, however, this project could never have been completed without the willing participation of a large number of clergy and church attenders. Not only was their completion of the questionnaire central to our endeavours, but some also played a major role in its distribution and collection at the many churches surveyed. To all these we are greatly indebted. Interaction with the attitudes of this substantial body of people in Belfast has been both enlightening and rewarding, and yet we are only too aware that they cannot be held accountable for the judgements we express and the interpretations we advance.

I

Introduction

On Monoliths

The Protestant and Catholic communities in Northern Ireland are frequently depicted as two, monolithic, opposing blocs. We believe that there are good reasons to suppose that this oppositional discourse exhibits a high degree of typecasting which fails to take seriously the real complexity inherent in the typically casual use of the term 'the two communities'.

The tendency towards monolithising ethnic 'others' has been the subject of a number of historical and sociological investigations. These have sought to uncover the range of contexts and strategies—both intentional and unintentional—through which discourses of difference have been produced. We are increasingly aware of just how common it is for external commentators to falsely portray, and thereby to reify, ethnically diverse communities as monolithically uniform. Two case studies are particularly illustrative. In his exploration of the black inner city, David Ley exposed the distorted white image of black Philadelphia as an internally coherent, revolutionary-prone, efficiently organised, racial monolith. Instead, investigations drawn from participant observation revealed that what had been thought of as a 'frontier outpost' was an unstable amalgam of ethnically diverse groups and gangs hostile to each other. As Ley concludes: 'There is no solidarity or consensus unique to the black inner city' (Ley, 1974, p. 242). A second case is Edward Said's historical scrutiny of 'Orientalism' (1978) in which he uncovered the complex array of rhetorical devices by which the West imposed a manipulative uniformity on 'the East.' In this critique he deconstructed the idea of the 'Orient' by demonstrating how it was produced politically, culturally, militarily, and imaginatively by the West during the post Enlightenment period. Through an amalgam of 'fact and fiction', which together produced an 'imaginative geography', the Orient was set off from Europe as a kind of alter ego. By this manoeuvre Said showed how spaces and places are 'produced' and presently become the locus of scholarly and other forms of interrogation.

No doubt processes and practices such as these have been evident within Northern Ireland. Consider, for example, the 'baffled disgust', as the Irish historian F.S.L. Lyons put it (1979b, p. 134), of outside observers which arises from their perplexed revulsion towards a situation which they see as primitive, endemic atavism. Even 'historians', to again quote Lyons, 'are inarticulate about the different cultures which collide with each other' in Ireland, and this, he claims, 'is merely a symptom of a more profound ignorance which runs through our society and is exhibited *in excelsis* on the other side of the Irish sea' (Lyons, 1979a, p. 14).

Perhaps reflecting these very sources is the suite of political theories advanced in an endeavour to make sense of the Irish situation. Among these are the discourses emanating from traditional Irish nationalists, Marxist social theorists of various stripes, advocates of two nations/two traditions and champions of the double minority model. Despite their varying theoretical orientations and political objectives, what unites these commentators is the unquestioned assumption that Northern Ireland houses two distinct communities. The upshot of all this is an all-too-frequent exasperation at the province's evident failure to comply with theoretical prescription.

Aspects of everyday life in Northern Ireland may well contribute to reinforcing the monolithic presupposition. High levels of residential segregation, separate educational structures, sectarian violence, different recreational pursuits, territorial behaviour, friendship networks, endogamy and, of course, patterns of church attendance all serve to sustain a belief in the existence of two monolithic blocs.

However analytically convenient or politically expedient the rudimentary taxonomy of 'two traditions' may be, we believe that there are good grounds for affirming that such stereotypical portrayals fail to do justice to reality. To subsume every aspect of social life and cultural identity under the bi-polar rubric of sectarian antithesis is to fall captive to a reductionism whose status is, at the very least, contestable. Such stereotypes are perpetuated from generation to generation. Accordingly, we believe the time is right to undertake an in-depth investigation of the 'two traditions'; only in this way can the cultural diversity that actually exists in Northern Ireland be more fully appreciated.

Space for Religion

There are, to be sure, different ways in which the received wisdom about two monoliths may be disputed, notably in terms of class, culture, and creed. In this project, however, we choose to focus on the religious arena not least because commentators (both secular and ecclesiastical) have all-too-frequently ignored or minimised the salience of religious sentiment in the Northern Ireland conflict, on some occasions in the interests of promoting political or economic interpretations. This does not mean, of course, that religious accounts are entirely absent. For example, O'Brien (1972, p. 307) felt drawn back to what he called the 'rather obvious fact of a conflict between groups defined by religion.' The previous year, Rose (1971, p. 248) had depicted Northern Ireland as a 'bi-confessional society.' And even those who assert that the conflict is not religious have sometimes conceded that it involves a 'sizeable religious component' (Galliher and DeGregory, 1985, p. 58). Nevertheless, the complexity of religious commitment and experience has remained largely unexplored. Even those advocating the central significance of religious factors typically present the problem in terms of bi-polar religious monoliths. In large measure it is precisely because interpretations of Northern Irish society have been dominated by a conflictual model of social life that Protestants and Catholics have been stereotypically portrayed as occupying monochrome oppositional camps.

How might we begin to question these monolithic stereotypes? One way is to examine the variety of religious spaces—both material and metaphysical—which are occupied by significant numbers of people in Northern Ireland. The sites of religious practice—church, chapel, hall—are highly significant arenas in which key aspects of social reproduction are effected. In these places, values, attitudes, and practices are promulgated which have immensely significant ramifications in the taken-for-granted life-world of many people. In routinised ways, churchgoers come together at specified times to engage in a variety of religious and non-religious activities that condition everyday life. Many come to places of worship several times in a week; they bring their children to a variety of organisations; they engage in recreational activities with other church members; and many send their children to schools with particular religious values.

The specific church sites—material places—which constitute the arenas in which religious and social life are transacted, of course, do not exist in isolation from broader institutional religious structures. They are typically connected to other churches through parish and diocesan structures, systems of denominational organisation, and so on. At the least material, and most metaphysical end of the spectrum, are the belief spaces that religious practitioners occupy. Some are more orthodox or conservative in their outlook than others, and these stances over doctrine or practice condition the everyday lives of their advocates. Individual church, ecclesiastical, and belief spaces, moreover, do not exist outside the realm of other key elements of social life. They are, for example, connected in various ways to the neighbourhoods within which both churches and churchgoers are to be found. Besides, churchgoing frequently has ethnic significance, since ethnic identity often manifests itself in religious ways. Indeed there are those in Northern Ireland for whom church attendance is imbued with symbolic significance—what C.S. Lewis once referred to as the semi-political churchgoing of Ulster. Evidently an elucidation of religious spaces in the production and reproduction of social life is of considerable significance in understanding the nature of society in Northern Ireland. Religious space, then, is multi-dimensional space, material and metaphorical, physical and social, in which ideology, iconography, and sociability are explicitly and/or tacitly integrated.

Exploring the 'Monoliths'

In order to go beyond monolithic stereotypes, it is necessary to widen the scope of investigation beyond ecclesiastical policy, church structure and theological tradition by examining the behaviour, beliefs and values of ordinary church-going people. Thus the findings reported here are derived from a questionnaire-based survey of church-going Catholics and Protestants in Belfast, supplemented by in-depth interviews with clergy.[1] To be sure, an analysis of the entire Protestant and Catholic communities across Northern Ireland would be enlightening. But we have limited our study to Belfast churchgoers, not only because this restriction increased the project's manageability, but also because of the coherence and significance of these particular groups. Whatever the drawbacks of this limitation, it has enabled us to investigate with considerable precision and depth significant subsections of the Northern Ireland population, namely, church-going Catholics and Protestants in the Belfast urban area.

In the following pages we attend initially to internal differences and similarities among Catholic churchgoers using demographic, theological, moral, neighbourhood and political characteristics. Protestant churchgoers are similarly scrutinised in the succeeding chapter. We believe it is of fundamental importance to deal with each of these churchgoing populations separately, in the first instance, in

---

1. Details of research methodology, survey operation, analytical procedures, and a copy of the Protestant and Catholic questionnaires, are to be found in the Appendices.

order that their intrinsic authenticity may be maintained. Too frequently, as we have already indicated, these communities have only been examined in the light of each other, and routinely in oppositional terms. Such a perspective, we maintain, inevitably trades in the very stereotypes which it is our aim to transcend. We have therefore designed our analysis to ensure—as far as possible—that this objective is realised. Having said this, we believe it is also important to trace both continuities and discontinuities across this conventional divide, and accordingly chapter IV is devoted to elucidating these relationships.

The findings which follow are presented in the hope of making some small contribution both to the greater understanding of the role of religious belief and practice in this deeply troubled society, and to the querying of our complacent acceptance of a religiously defined 'them and us' divide.

II

Catholic Churchgoers

General Introduction

Visitors to Belfast are impressed by the levels of activity at churches on Sunday mornings.[1] This distinguishes Catholic churches here from their counterparts elsewhere in Europe.[2] The data that we have gathered indicate, however, that in other respects Belfast's churchgoing Catholics follow general late twentieth century trends: they are more likely to be women (60%), to be middle-aged and elderly (two-thirds are over 45 and a third are over 65) and to have among them only small numbers of young people under 25 (7%). The whole spectrum of educational levels is represented (39% have only had a primary education, while 17% have a third level education[3]). They are, however, just as likely to be from manual (51%) as from non-manual (49%) occupational backgrounds. Nevertheless, there are few unemployed present despite the fact that Catholic unemployment in Belfast is above average.[4]

These similarities with other countries have emerged in the context of the almost universal changes in society that have slowly pervaded

---

1. 85% of Catholics in Northern Ireland attend Mass at least once a week (European Values Survey, 1990); 75% of Catholics in Belfast are regular churchgoers (Continuous Household Survey, 1988-91).
2. European average for Catholic attendance at least once a week is only 42% (European Values Survey, 1990).
3. The Northern Ireland average for Catholics with a third level education is 11% (Continuous Household Survey, 1988-91).
4. 24% of economically active Catholics are unemployed compared to 17% overall for Belfast (Census of Population, 1991).

Western Europe. The process of modernisation, with its inevitable societal and cultural ramifications, has gradually modified religious meanings. Attendant secularisation, accelerating since the 1960s, has been facilitated by increased mobility and access to other worlds by media coverage and the immediacy of television. Such new ideas have steadily eroded traditional relationships based on respect for order, authority and certainty. Furthermore, as a consumer culture has taken root and as scientific explanation has replaced theological, often fatalistic, explanations for society's phenomena, there has been a weakening of a religious world-view characterised by a respect for organised religion, its institutions and practices. Conformist views on marriage, family matters and gender roles are rapidly giving way to an increasing societal tolerance of individualistic views on most matters. These transformations have not bypassed Belfast's Catholics.

Indeed, the Catholic Church itself has not remained unaltered; internal renewal since the Second Vatican Council (1962-65) has been a major influence in opening up to many Catholics the possibility of a private world of conscience, has affirmed a more widespread participation of the 'people of God' in church life, and has slowly freed them from unquestioning obedience to rules and instructions dictated from above. Vatican II has also liberated religious thinking from a focus on the wrath of God to one which is more forgiving and optimistic. What is more, Vatican II has affirmed ecumenism. Its overall impact has been, inevitably, to differentiate those Catholics whose religious consciousness was formed prior to these societal and ecclesiastical changes from their younger co-religionists.

In many respects, however, the liturgical reform and ecumenical openness of Vatican II has been enacted often more to the letter, rather than in the spirit, of the law in Ireland where the Catholic Church has been, for generations, the central organising principle of life for faithful, passive Catholics who obeyed its teachings unquestioningly. A model of the Irish Church based on the sacraments has remained strong and it has stood steadfast as a clerical church which is perceived and experienced as male and hierarchical. Nonetheless, even here it has been unable to withstand the liberalising challenges of the late twentieth century.

Other local concerns have also coloured the experiences of Belfast's Catholics and may have contributed to fragmenting the Church. For example, almost all have been affected to some degree by the severe economic and political tensions during the last thirty years, and these conditions have made a deep impression on the values and attitudes of many Northern Irish Catholics. Large scale job losses, added to traditionally high levels of unemployment among Catholics, have led to the marginalisation of some as an underclass for whom persistent long-term unemployment has become a way of life. In sharp contrast, others have prospered, many being able to take advantage of the educational opportunities and the consequent possibilities for upward social mobility which have been afforded since the 1950s. All, however, have felt the strains of political upheaval, as behaviour associated with inter-ethnic conflict has become the norm in Northern Irish society. Death and injury have affected substantial numbers of both Catholics and Protestants, for over 3,000 people have died and another 37,000 have been injured as a consequence of conflict during the last twenty-five years. Furthermore, at least 15,000 households in Belfast were driven from their homes, either by bomb-damage or intimidation, during the 1970s alone in what has been one of the biggest population movements in Western Europe since the Second World War (Keane, 1990). To some of its adherents the Catholic Church stands accused of having distanced itself from their problems and of failing to condemn oppression in sufficiently strong terms whilst being apparently ready to condemn violence.

In the light of these local divergent factors the wider modernising and secularising trends experienced elsewhere have been tempered. Accordingly, a more fragmented Catholic population might be expected today. Furthermore, since the values and attitudes that influence behaviour are largely fashioned in the formative years of life it might be expected that differences will emerge between those raised amidst such forces and those brought up in the more traditional world before the 1960s, when order, authority and certainty reigned. Such fragmentation will become evident in the different values and attitudes that people show towards religion, morality, social concerns and community tensions. In addition, it will be reflected in concepts of identity and political outlook. We would, of course, expect to find unifying as well as divergent strands, yet not such as would contribute to the monolithic status often ascribed to Catholics by those outside the Catholic Church. The data we have gathered on their religious behaviour and convictions and their social and political attitudes challenge this ascription and suggest a diversity among Catholic churchgoers which we will now explore. With this in mind we turn first to Catholic religious life.

Religious Practice And Beliefs

There are several elements in the religious behaviour and belief of Catholics. The first element is practice, which concerns the extent to which Catholics attend to sacramental duties, prayer life, the Scriptures and other pious devotions. However, since practice does not necessarily mean commitment to Catholic beliefs, attitudes to particular church teachings and the strength of those beliefs are also important. Beliefs, then, as well as religious practice, are scrutinised.

Practice
The underpinning to our work is the assumption, following the Catholic sacramental model, that a practising church is a healthy church. Our survey included questions on all aspects of religious practice such as attendance at Mass and other Sacraments, attention to prayer, scripture reading and participation in certain other devotions. Responses indicate a body of Catholic churchgoers who are far from uniform in their practice.

Sacramental Participation
The evidence makes it clear that Belfast's Catholic churchgoers take seriously the Sunday church attendance obligation, the minimum criterion of a practising Catholic. Attendance at Mass, the Sacrament of the

Eucharist, at least once a week is almost universal. Half of the respondents, moreover, attend Mass more frequently, over a quarter daily. These people are almost all communicants on these occasions. Such comforting mass attendance figures, among the highest in Western Europe,[5] may camouflage other trends in sacramental participation. For example, fewer people receive Holy Communion than are present at Mass. Only three-quarters receive weekly in spite of such high mass attendance. This may be a reflection of scrupulousness, in the absence of a formal confession of sin before taking Communion, a tradition of pre-Vatican II days before Confession changed from an emphasis on penance to one of reconciliation. Alternatively, it may be a reflection of individual non-acceptance of some church teachings, of indifference, or even lack of belief.

Attendance at Confession (Sacrament of Reconciliation) is certainly now less frequent than attendance at Mass or Holy Communion.[6] While just over 30% of our churchgoers confess their sins at least once a month, 10% did not meet the minimum norm demanded by the Church, in that they never confessed at all or else did so less often than once a year. This movement away from the Sacrament of Reconciliation suggests a growing tendency for individual interpretations of sin and morality and the development of individual codes of moral behaviour. It also represents a move away from pre-Vatican II concepts which engendered fear of damnation and the need to make up through formal confessing and doing penance for every small transgression.

Nonetheless, there is no denying a very strong participation in the sacramental life of the Church and this points to an apparent solidity of practice among Catholics. However, even for those who attend Mass daily, only half consider that it is 'always wrong' to miss Sunday Mass and this attitude to the Sunday attendance obligation drops to 14%

---

5. Figures already noted in Footnotes 1 and 2.
6. MacGreil (1991) also found that, while church attendance remained high, there was a decline in attendance at Confession.

among those who do not fulfil it. Thus, the healthy appearance created by attendance figures may conceal considerable behavioural diversity among churchgoers. In order to explore this, a further analysis was made of attendance rates according to age, gender, education, occupational background and employment status.

Age

In general, young people are most noticeable by their absence (only 7% of respondents are 16-25) and, as Figure 1 shows, frequency of attendance at the Sacraments is closely related to age. The 18 to 24

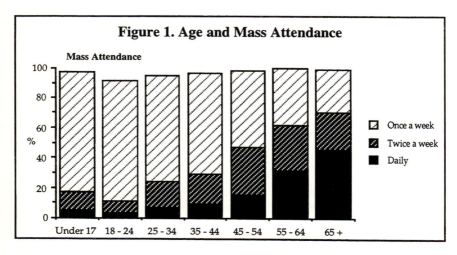

year old churchgoers stand out as the least frequent attenders at Mass and at Confession—indeed 17% *never* go to Confession. Furthermore, only the 25 to 34 year olds received Holy Communion less frequently.

In spite of this, it should be noted that those aged 17 or under appear to be slightly more rigorous in their attention to the Sacraments. Whether this represents a group strongly influenced by parents, by school, by social convenience or by spiritual conviction is unclear. In general what is clear is that younger Catholics are less likely to be at Mass and that when they are there they are likely to be the least

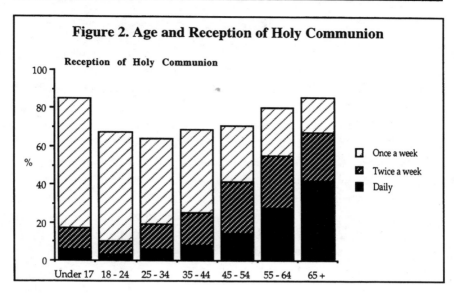

frequent attenders at Holy Communion. This evidence strongly suggests that growing up these days means growing away from religious practice.

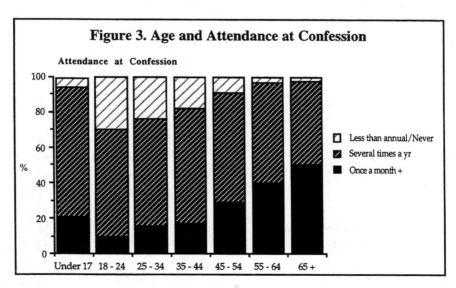

Differences between those under and over 45 were also marked. In respect of the Sacrament of Reconciliation, 42% of the over 45s go once a month or more compared to only 16% of those under 45. Indeed, this practice is reflective of their views on Confession. Doubt or rejection of its efficacy is highest among the younger churchgoers for only 72% of the under 45s firmly believe that sins are forgiven in Confession. In contrast, almost all of those over 45 (92%) are firm believers. Differences between the two groups may be explained by the differing social and religious environments of their religious formation. The older age group actually includes large numbers of the over 65s, nearly half of whom go to Mass daily. However, such a pattern of behaviour may also reflect life cycle reasons (religious consciousness often sharpens as Heaven draws near, greater opportunity exists or there is increased usage of the Church by older people as a centre for social interaction). Alternatively, it may be interpreted as symptomatic of a generational shift as religion takes on new meaning or is even rejected by younger people.

Education
Patterns of religious behaviour may, of course, be linked to differing levels of education. Is greater exposure to education, and the creation of supposedly more independent-minded people, having a negative effect on religious practice? Certainly, the most frequent Mass attenders have been educated only to primary level, although this may reflect age and the educational opportunities available in their youth. Among the over 45s more than a half are educated only to primary level (55%) compared to only 5% of the under 45s and the contrast between the two groups in university education is also marked (11% and 31% respectively). It is noticeable that as the proportion of those with a university education increases, the frequency of attendance decreases. Furthermore, it is the university educated who are the least likely to be frequent attenders at Confession; 19% do not fulfil the Church requirement compared to only 4% of those who are primary educated. The university educated are also less likely to believe that sins are forgiven in Confession (75%) which is an almost universal belief among the

primary educated (95%). But, as already observed, the impact of education may be linked to age.

Occupational Background

Different patterns of behaviour also emerge when the occupational background of churchgoers is considered. Those in manual occupations are less likely to take Communion, yet more likely to go to Confession at least monthly, than their co-religionists in professional/managerial occupations (48% and 18% respectively). If occupational difference is linked to education this would further suggest that the effective regulation of behaviour by Church ruling diminishes and individualised religious thinking increases with educational attainment.

Employment Status

The very reduced rate of church participation among the unemployed merits particular attention. Since Belfast is a city with a long history of persistent unemployment (rates in some areas sampled are as high as 80%) we would expect this unemployed population to be well represented among our churchgoers. However, they represent only 6% of respondents among whom 4% are long-term unemployed. These low levels of practice by the unemployed have been found elsewhere and Whelan (1994) suggests they may be associated more with a lowering of self-esteem and a consequent discomfort with being in a community situation, rather than any disaffection from the Church. Indeed, considering the unemployed who are Mass attenders, no difference overall is observable between them and the employed. However, they are noticeably less frequent communicants; 58% of them compared with 71% of those in employment, receive Communion once a week or more. Surprisingly, they are almost twice as likely as the employed to attend Confession at least once a month (37% compared to 20%).

Gender

A comparison of religious behaviour by gender is also worth considering. Whilst the most frequent attenders at Mass, Communion and Confession are female, differences in practice between the sexes are only very slight compared to differences by age, education and employment status. Differences are more obvious, however, between working women and those who look after the home; the latter are far more likely to attend Mass more than once a week (51% as compared to 37%) and a similar trend is obvious for those going to Communion and Confession. Why should this be so? It may reflect a difference of opportunity or educational level, the implications of which for religious practice are discussed above. However, it may also reflect, as some commentators have noted (Whelan, 1994), the secularising impact on working women of integration into the world of work. If so, this has implications for a society where female activity rates are increasing.

Sacramentals
In addition to participation in the sacramental life of the Church there is a Catholic tradition of engaging in other devotional practices. These are referred to as sacramentals and are used, according to the Catechism, 'in imitation of the Sacraments, to obtain from God spiritual favours'. These practices include praying to certain saints for intercession, making novenas,[7] doing the Stations of the Cross,[8] going on pilgrimages, the wearing of medals and scapulars,[9] the use of relics and the use of holy water in the home. The performance of such practices, which have their roots in traditional society, has often been taken as a sign of devotional piety, though others would regard it as superstitious (Inglis, 1987).

We have explored, therefore, the occurrence of such devotional practices as an indicator of adherence to tradition among Belfast's Catholic churchgoers. Although no attempt was made to measure frequency of practice it was found that, in general, such expressions of

---

7. Devotion consisting of prayers or services on nine consecutive days.
8. A series of fourteen representations of successive incidents from the Passion of Christ, visited in sequence for prayer and mediation.
9. Two pieces of cloth worn in imitation of Christ's yoke.

devotion are popular regardless of age and educational level. However, they were consistently more favoured by women. Prayer to special saints to intercede with God for favours and the use of holy water at home are the most widespread and involve almost three-quarters of churchgoers at least sometimes. Less popular, but still practised by 22%, is the occasional making of the Stations of the Cross. Furthermore, a half of those surveyed still wear medals, although very few claim to wear scapulars (13%) and this latter group is concentrated in the older age groups and among those of manual occupational backgrounds.

Given that frequency was not considered, an overall measure of devotional piety was obtained by comparing levels of usage on a scale from 'not used at all' to the 'use of all four' of the following practices: praying to special saints, wearing medals, wearing scapulars and making the Stations of the Cross. Overall, only 17% excluded these practices from their religious life. A third each used one or two of these expressions of piety. This figure dropped quite sharply to 14% who claim to use three and again dropped to only 5% who did all four.

An examination of the characteristics of these groups revealed that the most devotionally pious were much more likely to be female and over 65 years old. This group included few university graduates (only 8% compared to 28% of those who took part in no such practices) and consequently there were few from the professional/managerial occupational class. The most devotionally pious were also most likely to be frequent participants at the Sacraments, in private prayer, and in Bible reading. Moreover, the unemployed showed a much greater likelihood of engaging in these private practices than the employed. Belfast's churchgoers in general, then, appear to have adhered to tradition. Indeed, what is surprising, considering the portrayal of such religious practices as superstitious (Inglis 1987), is that they cover such a wide range of age groups.

Prayer
Personal piety is expressed in other ways amongst Belfast's Catholics. Their commitment to personal prayer is strong; just over three-quarters

of churchgoers claimed to pray at least once a day and, indeed, almost a half met the minimum suggested by church teaching of praying twice a day. In contrast, only 2% claimed never to pray or else to pray only on special occasions. Once again older people prayed more often whether they were male or female. On the other hand it was noticeable that the 18-24 year olds were least likely to pray often.

Perhaps as a sign of societal change, the tradition of family prayer remains in only three out of ten churchgoing households. As might be expected, it is most likely to be found in the family-centred homes of the under 45s, whilst being relatively absent among older people whose children may be grown up. Furthermore, it is much more common in professional/managerial households (39%) than in the homes of the unskilled (18%). Whether or not this definition of family prayer included saying the Rosary is unclear, since the Rosary, though traditionally a family prayer, may also be recited individually. It is a prayer which six out of ten people say at some time in either context.

Scripture Reading
Private Scripture reading was not a tradition among Catholics before the 1960s. We would expect, therefore, that even today Bible reading and contemplation would not be commonplace among our churchgoers. It is not surprising then that, although a half read Scripture irregularly or on special occasions and 16% read it once a week, 37% never read the Scriptures at all. The regular readers are more likely to be female and, surprisingly, to be over 45 years old. Education levels may be linked to the frequency with which Scripture is read (see Figure 4); among those never reading the Bible the majority are educated to primary or secondary/intermediate level whilst of all educational groups it is the most literate—the university educated—who are most likely to read the Scriptures. Accordingly, then, the professional/managerial classes far outrank those of unskilled backgrounds as Bible readers (71% and 52% respectively). However, in spite of their socialisation in a post-Vatican II era during which Bible reading has been encouraged, it does not appear to have established itself as a

regular practice amongst the younger Catholics, for 40% of the under 45s never read the Bible at all compared to 35% of the over 45s.

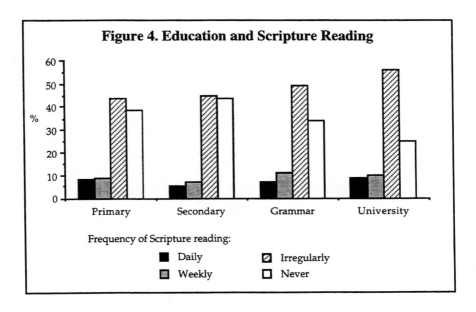

In sum, the levels of practice recorded in our survey suggest a very active church-going population, loyal to the sacraments, to prayer and other devotional practices. This, however, does not mean uniformity of behaviour. On closer scrutiny there are clear differences between those under and those over 45 years of age, the younger group being noticeably less diligent in their practice. What is more, this decided absence at church of younger people, especially those under 25, must be taken seriously. It is possible that life cycle reasons may be involved, but the signs are that a generational shift is taking place and the permanency of this shift seems likely given the major cultural changes of recent years. Whilst the bulk of our churchgoers retain, at least in their practice, a very dutiful, perhaps superstitious, approach to their religion, there is a component of individualism amongst those socialised after Vatican II, in a world where certainty, authority and order are no longer paramount. Furthermore, the absence of the socially marginalised, as evidenced by the small numbers of long-term unemployed, is noticeable and may also suggest a perception of the declining relevance of the Church to their lives.

Beliefs
Whilst patterns of practice are surface indicators of the varied spiritual health of Belfast's Catholic churchgoers, patterns of belief may be of more significance. Catholic beliefs reflect enduring Church teachings rather than the development of shared values and individual responsibility. Commitment to such teaching was assessed by looking at patterns of belief and at levels of orthodoxy. The importance of religion in the lives of individual churchgoers was also considered since this was regarded as an indicator both of individual commitment to the handing on of beliefs and values and of individual placing in theological space.

Patterns of Belief
An examination of belief patterns makes it clear that the commitment of Belfast Catholic churchgoers to the Church's central teachings was strong among both men and women. Almost everyone firmly believed in the Resurrection of Christ (93%) and even more affirmed that people can sin (97%). Belief in a life hereafter was also strong; over 80% firmly believed that there is a life after death, that the Devil exists and that there is a Heaven although fewer (75%) firmly believed in Hell. And of the Bible, 82% firmly accepted that it is the Word of God.

Other teachings considered were those related to the Sacraments; in such matters a firm belief in both transubstantiation and that sins are forgiven in Confession was evident (85%). In addition, the same high proportions firmly accepted the mariological teachings on the Immaculate Conception[10] and the Assumption of Our Lady into Heaven.[11] Nevertheless, taken overall, fewer believed that the Catholic Church is the one true church (74%) and fewer still accepted teaching on Papal Infallibility (62%). In spite of the similarity of belief patterns between men and women, uniformity of belief is not universal. Age, once again, appears to distinguish levels of commitment to most teachings, so that increasing age brings with it an increase in firmness of belief. A particularly wide variation exists between the young and old on the matters of Papal Infallibility and the Catholic Church being the one true Church (see Figures 5 and 6). This gap tends to confirm that there

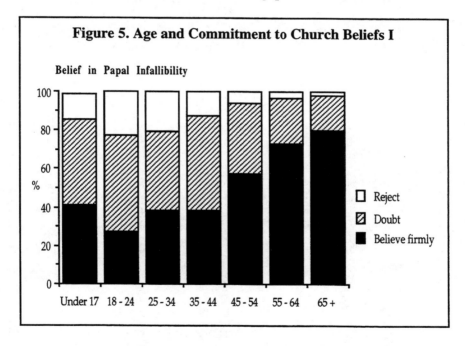

10. The Virgin Mary was conceived without the stain of original sin.
11. The Virgin Mary was assumed body and soul into Heaven.

is a weakening of the institutional Church as a spiritual and moral authority among younger Catholics.

Yet, as Figures 5 and 6 show, the under 17 year olds are more likely than their slightly older counterparts (the 18-24 year olds) to retain faith in the Church. Whilst on all other beliefs the youngest are least likely to be firm believers, this does not mean that they are highest in rejecting these teachings. Rather, they are more likely to doubt; nonetheless, as they grow older, they may follow the belief pattern of the 18 to 24 year olds who are highest in rejecting Church teachings. Murray (1990), noting what he considered to be the disturbing evidence of doubt on a large scale among the young after leaving school, suggests that it may be due to 'a failure of homes, parishes and communities to reinforce the work of the school' (pp. 77-8).

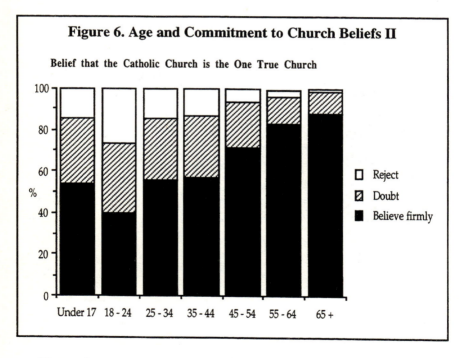

Not only age but also educational levels seem to distinguish between Catholics in respect of beliefs. Throughout, those educated to a higher standard were much less likely to be firm believers (Table 1) and most likely to reject the teachings of the Church, particularly those teachings on Papal Infallibility and the supremacy of the Catholic Church. Furthermore, those in manual occupational classes are consistently more likely than those people from non-manual occupational backgrounds to be firm believers in church teachings.

Table 1. Education and Belief Levels

	% believing firmly		
Belief	**Primary**	**Secondary**	**University**
The Bible is the Word of God	91	79	73
People can sin	99	97	94
The Devil exists	92	80	66
The Assumption	95	87	65
Papal Infallibility	81	55	35
The Catholic Church is the One True Church	89	72	48

The unemployed, commented on already as being a low practising group, were strong in their commitment to central beliefs in contrast to the employed (Breslin and Weafer, 1984; Fogarty *et al*, 1984). This supports the conclusion drawn by Whelan (1994) that low attendance by this group may be a sign of low self-esteem rather than disaffection with the Church or its teachings. However, the likelihood of this firmness in belief being linked to lower educational levels should also be considered.

Membership of the workforce is also reflected in the differences in commitment between women who are working outside the home and women who look after the home. Working women are below average in their commitment to the Church's central teachings, while those looking after the home are more committed.

Levels of Commitment

Whatever their beliefs, individual Catholics may differ in the overall strength of their convictions and thus levels of orthodoxy may vary. Such levels have been measured in previous surveys (Nic Ghiolla Phádraig, 1974; Breslin and Weafer, 1984) using a scale to place respondents in one of three orthodoxy categories, high, moderate or low, depending on commitment to basic church teachings. The Belfast survey, for comparative purposes, used the same technique and the same nine basic Catholic beliefs (see Table 2). Those 48% of churchgoers who believed firmly in all nine teachings are considered to be of high orthodoxy. However, those who expressed doubt in one to five are considered to be of moderate orthodoxy and represent 38% of our respondents. The remaining 14% of churchgoers expressed doubt on six to nine of the teachings and are, therefore, regarded as being of low orthodoxy.

Table 2. Orthodoxy and Belief Levels

Belief	% believing firmly		
	High	Moderate	Low
The Resurrection of Christ	100	97	52
The Bible is the Word of God	100	78	28
People can sin	100	97	86
The Assumption of the Blessed Virgin	100	91	15
The Immaculate Conception	100	92	19
Papal Infallibility	100	30	1
Sins are forgiven in Confession	100	87	31
Transubstantiation	100	88	21
The Catholic Church is the One True Church	100	60	15

These levels of orthodoxy are replicated in all aspects of practice and belief in church teachings so that, for example, those of highest commitment are also the most frequent attenders at the Sacraments. Conversely, frequency of attendance decreases as strength of conviction decreases. It is clear that, if their responses are to be believed, Belfast's Catholic churchgoers in general tend towards orthodoxy, rather than individualism.

A closer look at the variations in orthodoxy groups is instructive. The highly orthodox churchgoers are just as likely to be men as women, but are more likely to be over 45 (83%), to be educated only to primary level (54%) and to be in the manual occupational classes (54%). In contrast, as Figures 7 and 8 show, those of low orthodoxy,

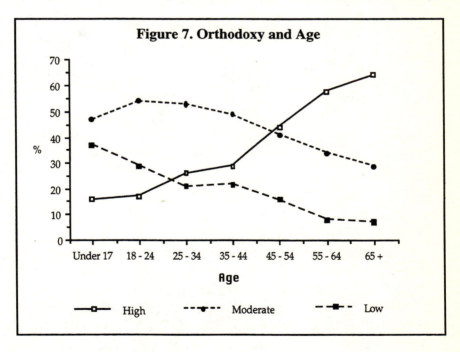

while slightly more likely to be female, are younger (55% under 45 years old), more highly educated (34% with University education compared to only 10% of the high orthodoxy group) and their occupations reflect this difference (three-fifths are non-manual). Those we have classified as moderate in their level of commitment lie somewhere between the higher and lower groups in all their characteristics. These general findings are confirmed by other surveys suggesting that the Belfast situation is part of a universal process (Breslin and Weafer, 1984).

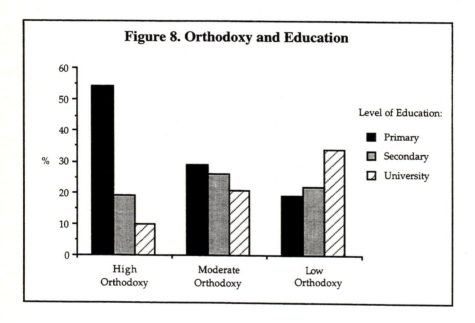

Since the low orthodoxy group may be closest in outlook to Catholic non-attenders it is thought worthwhile to describe their belief pattern in more detail. Less than a half of them shared a firm belief in any one church teaching, except for those on the existence of Sin (86%) and on the Resurrection (52%). Belief in life after death, in Heaven and in the Devil was held by around 38%, while only a quarter believed in Hell. This suggests that this group may be of a less pessimistic mindset than their co-religionists. Nearly one third accepted that sins are forgiven in Confession, yet a third either never went to Confession at all or else went less than once a year. Church teaching on transubstantiation presented a difficulty for 69% and indeed was totally rejected by a further 10%.

Mariological teachings were even less likely to be accepted; only a fifth believed in the Immaculate Conception and even fewer in the Assumption of the Blessed Virgin into Heaven. Belief levels dropped still further on the subject of the Catholic Church being the one true Church and, finally, belief in Papal Infallibility was negligible (1%). Members of this group, then, show a strong tendency to decide for themselves what they want to believe and this suggests an *à la carte* attitude to the teachings of the Catholic Church.

It is clear, then, that participation in Mass and the Sacraments can camouflage these differences of commitment. Weekly attendance at Mass is high among all groups (over 90%) but the low orthodoxy group was considerably less likely to attend frequently. As has already been shown they were also less likely to firmly believe in transubstantiation. Reception of Holy Communion followed the same pattern. As for Confession nearly one-third of those of lower orthodoxy, compared to 3% and 11% of the high and moderate orthodoxy groups respectively, did not fulfil the annual minimum attendance stipulated by the Catholic Church.

Unlike members of the low orthodoxy group, around eight out of ten of the moderate commitment group believe firmly in most of the teachings of the Catholic Church. The exceptions are that the Catholic Church is the one true Church, about which belief drops to six out of ten, and the infallibility of the Pope which is accepted by only three out of ten. This mixed pattern may be linked to their age and education; they represent over a half of under 45s and almost a half of the university educated. However, in general, these moderates tend more towards the levels of belief espoused by those of high, rather than of low, commitment.

The Role of Individual Conscience
Another approach to establishing differing levels of commitment to Catholic Church teachings is to look at what people consider to be the most important guide to living a Christian life. Scriptures and Church

teachings together are supposed to inform the practice and beliefs of Catholics, in contrast to either the individual's conscience or scriptures alone, as favoured by other Christian Churches. We found, nonetheless, that almost a half of all Belfast Catholic churchgoers considered individual conscience to be their most important guide (48%), slightly more than those committed to following scriptures and Church teachings (45%). Not unexpectedly, given Catholic tradition, only a small handful opted for scriptures alone (7%).

This overall picture shows the way in which surface obedience to rules can camouflage a growing individualism, especially among the younger groups (see Figure 9). The importance of individual

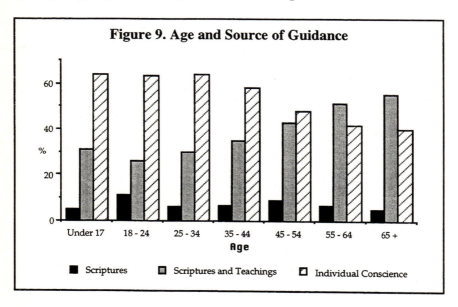

conscience was most frequently highlighted by those under 45 (61%). This underlines the generational shift already remarked upon since half of the over 45s consider their best guide to be scriptures and Church teachings together. In the light of the levels of commitment to particular church teachings expressed by the under 45s it seems that younger churchgoers value their own judgement rather than the authority of the Church. Furthermore, over three quarters of the low orthodoxy group highlighted the importance of individual conscience, compared to only a third of those of high orthodoxy. Indeed, when employment status was considered, only the retired group had a majority who conformed to the conventional Church wisdom on the guiding role of scriptures and Church teachings. Catholics in manual occupations were a little more likely than their non-manual co-religionists to follow conscience, though, surprisingly, education does not seem to matter in distinguishing individualism.

Importance of Religion
Commitment to the Catholic Church may also be gauged in other ways which have long term implications for religious practice and belief. One such method is to look at the importance of religion in churchgoers' lives. Church teaching suggests that membership of the Catholic Church should be either all or extremely important to them and, indeed, for three-quarters of churchgoers this was the case. However, the figure ranged from 90% for those of high orthodoxy to only 31% for the low orthodoxy group. Furthermore, as levels of education improve so the centrality of church membership in people's lives appears to wane. Among the primary educated, 82% considered membership of the Catholic Church to be all or extremely important compared to 64% of the university educated. Of greater significance is the fact that younger people are also less likely to feel that the Church is so central in their lives (see Table 3). For example, less than a half of the under 17s felt

Table 3. Age and Centrality of Church Membership

Membership of RC Church :	Under 45	Over 45
All Important/Extremely Important	57%	81%
Very Important/Important	38%	18%
Not Very Important/Not Important	5%	1%

that church membership was all or extremely important. This has major implications for the contemporary and future Church and for the handing on of the faith in a secularising society.

In an attempt to establish commitment to handing on the faith, we looked at attitudes to the importance of bringing up children as Catholics, to sending children to a Catholic school and to the importance of marrying a Catholic. Overall, only six out of ten considered that it was always wrong not to bring children up as Catholics. Once again sharp differences occurred between the over and under 45 year olds (66% and 42% respectively saw this as always wrong) and, what is more, the 18 to 24 year olds stand out as being those least likely to take this view (see Figure 10). How this is translated into the bringing up of children remains to be seen. In any event, their views are another strong pointer to the generational shift that is taking place. Moreover,

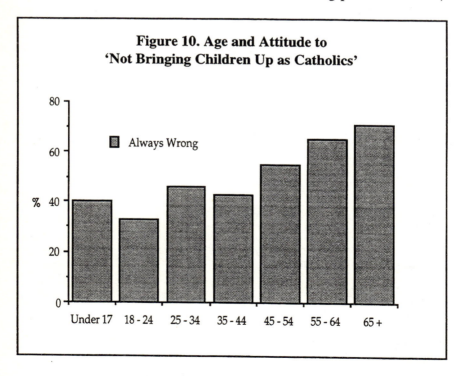

Figure 10. Age and Attitude to 'Not Bringing Children Up as Catholics'

the differences in outlook between society's leaders and the rest of the population stand out; differences were marked between those with a university education and those whose education finished at primary level and between those of non-manual and manual occupational classes. This picture is mirrored in attitudes to Catholic education. Whilst a third of churchgoers considered that it was always wrong not to send children to a Catholic school, age and education appear to moderate such views. Only one in ten of those who were university educated felt morally compelled to send their children to a Catholic school compared to over half of those whose education finished at primary school. Similarly those from manual occupational backgrounds emerged as being more scrupulous than their non-manual counterparts. Those of high orthodoxy are also much more likely to adhere to Church advice on education; half of them, compared to a tenth of the low orthodoxy group, are conformists.

As for marrying another Catholic, almost a fifth of our Catholic churchgoers did not consider it important. Nonetheless, attitudes varied according to age, a fact which may also be significant in the future, especially as over 40% of the under 25s adopted this stance.

To summarise then, Belfast's Catholic churchgoers are strong in the practice of their religion and currently follow the rules of the Church on such matters. It can be said, also, that they tend to be legalistic, and perhaps even superstitious, in some matters which would suggest a high degree of conformism and traditionalism. This conclusion was confirmed by Whelan (1994, p.35) when he described Northern Irish Catholics as retaining 'to a much greater extent than Catholics elsewhere in Europe, a traditional approach.' This observation is further supported by the fact that half of all respondents agreed that people were better off in the old days when they knew just how they were expected to act. This attitude confirms the importance that age and educational attainment have, more than anything else, in defining levels of traditionalism in religious practice.

An overall surface obedience to rules, however, hides considerable diversity in belief, a more significant factor in appreciating the state of religious life. We found that just less than a half of churchgoers had a high level of commitment to the central teachings of the Catholic Church and this diversity of belief was most noticeable in relation to teaching on the nature of the institution particularly with regard to Papal Infallibility. What is apparent is that a Catholic churchgoing population has emerged, especially among its younger, better educated members, which is no longer unquestioning of rules and teachings. Instead, it is more likely to exercise individual conscience in spite of church directives, although perhaps 'doing so, not because they have lost faith in God, but because they have lost hope in the Church' (O'Sullivan, 1994).

Moral and Social Concerns

It has already been noted that Belfast's Catholics have not escaped local manifestations of universal secularisation processes. Furthermore, local socio-economic and political concerns have provided the backdrop against which the changes of Vatican II have been enacted. These changes have influenced not only the Church as an institution but also the relationships between the Churches and the lives of individual Catholics. The impact of such changes, particularly in relation to roles within the Church and the relevance of religion to the lives of people, will now be examined.

The Church as an Institution

We chose, in the first place, to ask churchgoers about their attitudes to changes such as the roles played by the laity in general and, more specifically, played by women. We also asked about the relevance of the liturgy to their lives and their attitude to the nature of language used in the liturgy.

Lay Participation

Although lay participation has been limited to a few areas of life in the Catholic Church, the contribution of lay people in the distribution of Holy Communion has been a central feature of change. When questioned on their attitudes to this well-established practice, seven out of ten people approved both of lay eucharistic ministers at Mass and in the distribution of Holy Communion to the sick. The older respondents were just as likely as the young to be supportive, although the attitudes of those with a university education were much more favourable than those of the primary educated (87% agreed compared to 64%). Attitude differences between occupational classes are also evident. Those of a professional/managerial background are more likely to support lay eucharistic ministers than those churchgoers from unskilled backgrounds (85% compared to 58%). It is uncertain whether this middle-class attitude reflects, or whether it underlies, the domination of the lay contribution by this social class as readers, as eucharistic ministers and as parish group leaders. It can be concluded, nonetheless, that although there are varying strengths of support, any opportunity for lay people to participate is almost universally welcomed.

The Role of Women
A more contentious issue, however, is the role of women in the Church. Overall, just over half agreed that women do not have enough responsibility. Men and women do not differ in their views, although younger members of the congregation, the better educated, those in non-manual occupational classes and those of lower orthodoxy are much more likely to agree that women are underrepresented and undervalued.

More specifically, there was general agreement on the institution of female eucharistic ministers, no matter about the age, gender or orthodoxy of the respondent. The most approving were those with higher educational levels and those in professional/managerial occupations. As far as the topical issue of female altar-servers was concerned, over 60% overall favoured this innovation; those of low orthodoxy were far more likely to be supportive (81% compared to 53% of the high orthodox). However, we found that churchgoers were more uncertain in their views about the ordination of women; just under one-quarter of them, whether male or female, were convinced. Once again the main differences between those agreeing and those disagreeing with

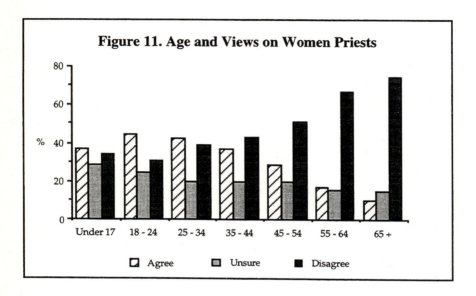

Figure 11. Age and Views on Women Priests

the ordination of women were related to age (see Figure 11), education, occupational background and orthodoxy, with around 30 percentage points of difference between the extremes in all cases.

Relevance of Liturgy
We turn now to liturgical matters and to preaching. Attitudes to the relevance of sermons to the lives of people were considered. It was generally agreed by three-quarters of churchgoers, irrespective of sex, age, education or orthodoxy, that sermons should on some occasions deal with social and economic problems. There was also interest shown towards having some sermons dealing with political problems. Although, overall, six out of ten agreed, irrespective of gender or occupational background, members of the 25-34 year old age group and the university educated were the most likely to express this view. The Church is clearly faced with mixed opinions on its role in political matters, a point to be considered later.

The language that is used in church is also a matter of contention in the 1990s. Therefore, we asked churchgoers if they would prefer the use of 'man' or 'humankind'. Surprisingly, not only did six out of ten

pared to 16% of those in employment. To summarise, those most strongly against artificial contraception are characteristically high in orthodoxy, older, lower educated, from manual occupational backgrounds or are unemployed. Even then no more than a half of these Belfast Catholic churchgoers follow Church teaching on this matter.

On the subject of abortion, however, there is a much more universal condemnation; nearly eight out of ten churchgoers (79%) consider it to be always morally wrong. Once again it is the older, less well educated and most orthodox who are much more likely to take this stance (see Table 5).

Table 5. Views on the Moral Issue of Abortion

		'Always Wrong'
Sex :	Male	80%
	Female	78%
Age :	Under 45	64%
	45 or over	86%
Orthodoxy :	High	93%
	Low	43%
Education :	Primary	91%
	University	66%
Occupation :	Professional/managerial	71%
	Unskilled	82%
Employment Status :	Employed	71%
	Unemployed	76%

However, attitudes are rather different when it comes to making abortion *legally* available, for only 45% of Catholics are against providing such an opportunity in any circumstances. The remaining 55% consider legalised abortion appropriate under certain circumstances. Such circumstances included it being the only way to save the mother's life (44%), when the pregnancy was the result of rape (33%) and when the child was likely to be born severely physically handicapped (15%). In all these cases the youngest age groups were most likely to approve while those with a primary education were least likely to approve. Of course the close link already observed between education and age should be remembered.

Such contingent attitudes are also apparent among Belfast's Catholic churchgoers as regards divorce. The Catholic Church has long frowned on civil divorce, but is prepared to accept it provided that there is no remarriage. In our survey more than a fifth of respondents stated that there were no circumstances in which civil divorce would be acceptable. This left around four fifths (78%) finding it acceptable in some context. Table 6 indicates attitudes to some such circumstances and it makes clear that the majority consider the occurrence of physical violence (61%) or of mental cruelty (58%) to be the most acceptable circumstances to warrant divorce. As with so many issues reported thus far, younger people appear to be less resistant to the idea of divorce. Among respondents 28% of over 45s compared to only 10% of those under 45 are firmly set against it.

Table 6. Circumstances in which Civil Divorce is Acceptable

Circumstances	% of Catholics agreeing
When physical violence occurs	61%
When mental cruelty occurs	58%
When desertion occurs	48%
When the marriage breaks down	43%
When adultery is committed	33%
When the partners are not suited	27%

Divorce also appears to be more acceptable to the better educated as only 12% of those with a university education are totally opposed to it compared to 34% of the primary educated. Furthermore, occupational class distinguishes attitudes as only 15% of those from a professional/

managerial background do not find divorce acceptable compared to 32% of those from an unskilled background.

To summarise, then, it is clear from the above evidence that Belfast's Catholic churchgoers still generally conform to Church teachings on private morality. Nonetheless, a growing individualism is exhibited by the younger, better educated, higher status members of society who appear to make up their own minds about what is morally acceptable. Entry into the labour force and exposure to secularising ideas may well be contributing factors. It should be noted, for example, that women in work were found to be consistently more liberal on moral matters than were those looking after the home (on the issue of sex before marriage, only 43% of those employed found this to be always wrong compared to 60% of those in the home). What emerges overall is the declining influence of the authority of Church teaching in all matters of personal morality.

Attitudes to Discipline
Churchgoing Catholics were also asked to express their views on a range of issues concerned with morality in the public arena, specifically on discipline and punishment in school and in the courts. Their attitudes to capital punishment were also sought. Almost six out of ten agreed with bringing back the cane into schools (57%), although the over 45 year olds are its greatest advocates. Personal experience and recent media coverage of increasing criminal activity may account for 81% agreeing that the courts are too lenient; by contrast, only around a quarter (26%) agree with capital punishment.

Responses to these three questions were combined to produce a four-point public morality scale,[12] ranging from 'conservative' through 'conservative/moderate' to 'moderate/liberal' and 'liberal'. This reveals that church-going Catholics are middle-of-the-road types who fall into the middle two categories (71%). They are, however, a little more

---

12. See Appendix IV.

likely to have liberal tendencies, perhaps reflecting the less rigid, more forgiving tradition of post-Vatican II theology. As might be expected, those churchgoers with liberal views are more likely to be younger (three-quarters of them are under 55 years old), to be more highly educated (40% have a university education), to be in non-manual occupations (54%) and to be female (62%). On the other hand, the strict conservatives are likely to be male, to be primary educated, to be in manual occupations and to be aged 55 or over. The positive relationship between age and social conservatism can be seen clearly in Figure 12. Although the largest proportion of Catholic churchgoers of all ages fall into the 'moderate to liberal' category this proportion decreases with increasing age. Bearing in mind the important effect that experience has on attitude formation it is uncertain whether the younger liberals will retain these views as they grow older.

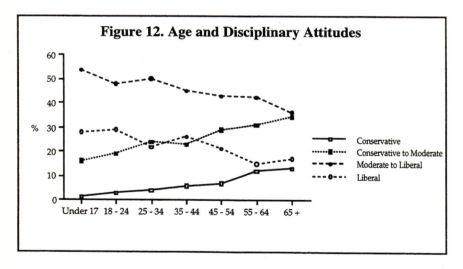

Education levels may have an even more marked influence than age on social attitudes (see Figure 13). It is clear that those with a university education are far less likely to be strict disciplinarians; nearly eight out of ten of them fall into the two more liberal categories in contrast to less than a half of those whose education finished at primary school, although it must once again be borne in mind that there is a link between age and education. The views of people from different occupational backgrounds may also reflect their education; those of non-manual occupations emerge less disciplinarian than people from a manual background.

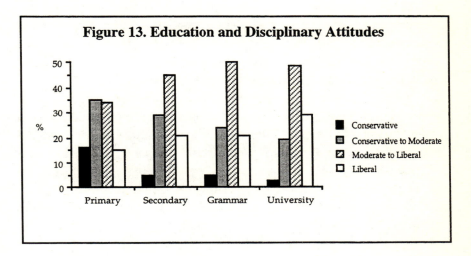

It is interesting to note, moreover, that there is a link between differing social attitudes and religious practice and belief. Churchgoers at the conservative end of our scale are distinguished by being the most orthodox and the most frequent attenders at Mass and the Sacraments. They are also actively involved in a range of traditional devotional activities. In contrast, the more liberal types are less frequent attenders. For example, those attending confession least frequently range from 18% at the liberal end of the social scale to 6% at the conservative end.

Finally, the observed differences in social attitudes are further reflected in differences in moral attitudes; those who are socially conservative tend also to be morally conservative.[13] For example differences between conservatives and liberals are as high as 50% in

---

13. See Appendix IV.

attitudes to pre-marital sex, co-habitation, abortion and homosexual practices.

Gender Roles

We now consider one of the more contentious contemporary concerns, at household level and in society in general. This has been the challenging of established gender roles. The idea that a woman's place is in the home and that men are the providers has been contested as more and more women have become part of the workforce.

Our churchgoers' attitudes to such changes were explored by asking them whether there were any circumstances in which they considered it right for a woman to go out to work. It appears that Catholic attitudes in this respect are generally non-traditional in that only 4% of our churchgoers considered that a woman's place is in the home. The vast majority (86%) were happy, for whatever reason, that women without children or with grown-up children could go out to work. The more difficult area, however, is when younger children are involved; although over a half approved of women working, even if they have school-age children, only a third considered work to be acceptable for those with children not yet at school. The majority of this latter group are themselves women (65%) and are younger (79% under 55 years old). They are also the better educated (31% have a university education) and are most likely to be from non-manual backgrounds (56%). It is interesting that these same people indicate a general approval for a breakdown in other traditional gender roles so that, for example, they are more likely to consider that women are not given enough responsibility in the Church and to approve the ordination of women priests (41% agree compared to the average figure of 23%). Furthermore, they are to be found among the more morally liberal Catholic churchgoers and few of them are highly orthodox in their commitment to church teachings. Socially they are clustered at the liberal end of the social conservatism scale (76%).

Non-traditional attitudes also carry through to views on responsibility in the home for 'holding the purse strings.' An overwhelming 84%

favoured a joint approach to money management and only 2% supported the husband taking charge of finances. While the traditional scenario has been for the husband to provide and for the wife to budget, only 14% still support this custom. Even then it is interesting that these people are older, mainly male, manual workers, whose education finished at primary level. They are the most likely to agree with the certainties of the old days (71% agree) and two-thirds are highly committed to all central teachings of the Catholic Church. In fact, they also consider that in church life women already have enough responsibility.

Our survey confirms that the Catholic conservatives, whether in matters of morals, discipline or gender issues, favour tradition as a touchstone of behaviour while the liberals, on the other hand, are more individualistic. In general, then, the two groups can be distinguished from one another both by adherence to traditional societal attitudes and by traditional religious views and practices. However, whether the existence of a conservative core on religious matters indicates spiritual commitment or social conformism is uncertain. In any event the implications of divergent outlooks for social mixing will now be considered.

Social And Religious Mixing

Vatican II, frequently referred to as the 'Ecumenical Council', urged Catholics to strengthen relationships with other denominations. Matters of ecumenism have, then, exercised the minds of Catholic Church leaders everywhere over the last twenty-five years. In Northern Ireland, where relations between Protestants and Catholics are of particular significance for people's lives, the local pressures and responsibilities have weighed even more heavily. Since the late 1960s the churches have addressed themselves to bridging centuries-old chasms which are defined not only theologically but also politically. Politicians have themselves either supported or discouraged in varying degrees such mixing which may take several forms, both social and religious.

Religious Mixing

Since church members may not necessarily follow the injunctions of their church leaders on ecumenism we explored the attitudes of these ordinary churchgoers. However, support among Catholic churchgoers for ecumenism is almost universal (99%), although attitudes towards the acceptable degree of religious mixing vary. Overall, nine out of ten Catholics thought that the Protestant and Catholic churches should aim either for unity or for greater co-operation in religious and social matters (47% and 46% respectively), leaving only 6% who thought the churches should only aim for co-operation on social matters; only 1% thought that there should be no co-operation whatsoever.

Older and primary-educated people were more likely to want the churches to aim for *unity* whilst younger people favoured *co-operation*. That this may reflect different concepts of unity is suggested by the fact that those of high orthodoxy were the most supportive of outright unity. What this means to them is not exactly clear since to be considered highly orthodox this group *had* to firmly believe that the Catholic church is the one true church. This group may well conceive of unity as a return to the Catholic fold by the 'separated brethren'. Nonetheless, whatever their understanding, almost all Catholics are committed to some form of religious co-operation at the very least.

Although 99% of respondents had always been Catholic these attitudes were not based on unsubstantiated perceptions; almost half of all Catholic churchgoers had attended an ecumenical service of Catholics and Protestants and this was just as likely an occurrence for the most committed as for the least committed Catholics. What is more, these joint services appear to attract all age groups, although those with higher levels of education and those from non-manual occupational backgrounds are more likely participants. However, this pattern may be explained by available opportunities in their neighbourhood. This is not to say that those who have not yet attended a joint service are unhappy to do so; such reservations were expressed by only 15% of all Catholic respondents.

Cross-community contacts can, of course, be made outside of joint worship, yet less than a fifth of churchgoers reported involvement in any kind of cross-community organisation. Moreover, only 2% had been involved in such an organisation associated with the Church. This is a point worth noting especially since two-thirds of all Catholic churchgoers consider that the Churches should be much more active in improving relations between the communities in Northern Ireland.

Social Mixing
And what of mixing in more social situations? Mixing on a social basis is more immediate in its impact and may have more significant structural implications for relationships between groups. However, attitudes to such mixing can vary depending on the social distance between the groups involved. A technique to measure social distance was devised by Bogardus (1925). In this study, willingness to mix was measured using an adaptation of the Bogardus Social Distance Scale[14] which assumes that the degree to which mixing is attractive varies according to the social intimacy involved. Situations were considered, ranging from having no dealings at all with the other group to links at work, as immediate neighbours through to the closeness of marriage. Attitudes to arrangements for the education of children were considered separately. Reactions to six groups, other than Northern Irish Catholics, in respect of these circumstances were examined. The groups were Black, Indian, Chinese, English, Southern Irish and Northern Irish Protestants. As expected, the less intimate the relationship inquired about, the greater the willingness of Catholics to mix. In

---

14. The Bogardus Social Distance Scale was originally a seven step scale used to measure intergroup attitudes and from which the respondent chooses the level closest to which he/she is prepared to admit a member of an out-group. Agreement to a degree of closeness presumes acceptance also of lesser degrees. Our adaptation asked for attitudes at four specific levels: marriage, neighbour, work and no dealings.

contrast, the closer the relationship involved, for example the intimacy of marriage, the less comfortable they were with mixing.

Catholics have fairly similar attitudes to Blacks, Chinese and Indians. Three-quarters of churchgoers are happy to work with such groups, almost two-thirds are willing to have them as neighbours but only a quarter expressed a willingness to marry them. It is of interest to observe that, of the three groups, Blacks are favoured slightly more than the other two (see Figure 14) in all situations.

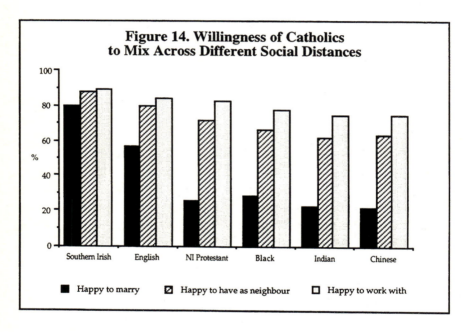

A much greater willingness to be involved with white groups is generally apparent, although ranking still exists. This is especially evident when it comes to acceptability as marriage partners since eight out of ten Catholics are happy with those from the Republic of Ireland compared to only six out of ten willing to intermarry with the English. This difference may be due to a greater familiarity with Southern Irish people as well the high likelihood that the Southern Irish share religion and identity.

In contrast to this, the willingness of Catholics to marry a Northern Irish Protestant (26%) falls closer to the levels for the three non-white groups. Indeed, Black marriage partners were marginally more acceptable (28%). This is despite the greater likelihood of relatively close geographical proximity, a degree of shared heritage and shared soil. Nonetheless, there were very few (only 3%) who indicated a complete unwillingness to mix with Protestants, or indeed any of the other groups. However, differences in age, sex, education and occupational background produce clear differences in attitudes to mixing at all levels of social intimacy and with all groups. For example, the 18 to 24 year old age group is proportionately most likely to agree to mixed marriage, to being neighbours and to working with the non-white groups. In contrast, of those who were resistant to mixing, a half were over 65 years old and had finished their education at primary level. These people are generally the most socially and morally conservative. They are also the most traditional in their commitment to Catholic teachings.

Work
It is at work that Catholics, both men and women, feel happiest about mixing with all groups, including Protestants. There are, however, differences in attitudes. As Table 7 shows there is more of a resistance to mixed working environments from the older members of the population. Despite this, even three-quarters of the retired age group would be happy to share a workplace with Southern Irish, English or Northern Irish Protestants and just over a half of them are happy to work with Blacks, Indians or Chinese, groups with whom they may have little familiarity. Any reticence shown to working alongside Northern Irish Protestants may reflect a history of employment or unemployment marred by perceived discrimination. This group also has amongst it large numbers of the most highly orthodox Catholics who are much less likely than those of lower orthodoxy to feel comfortable in a mixed working environment. In contrast, the young people (under 25s) were almost universally happy to work with all groups. This open attitude may be contributed to by the current paucity of employment

opportunities in Belfast. Not unexpectedly, moreover, those with a university education and those from non-manual backgrounds show themselves to be happy working with people from any group.

Table 7. Attitudes to mixing at work

	Per cent happy to work with					
	Southern Irish	English	N.I. Prot.	Black	Indian	Chinese
Sex : Male	90	84	82	77	73	73
Female	89	85	84	78	75	75
Age : 18 - 24	97	96	96	95	91	93
65 or over	78	72	72	58	55	54
Orthodoxy : High	85	78	77	69	66	66
Low	94	91	91	87	84	85
Education : Primary	81	74	73	64	60	59
University	97	95	96	93	90	90
Occupation : Unskilled	86	76	76	74	68	67
Prof/Managerial	96	93	93	87	86	86
Total Population	89	84	83	77	74	74

Neighbours

Attitudes to residential mixing have far reaching implications for Belfast and Northern Ireland society. It must be remembered that, as they perceive it, the majority of respondents live in 'all Catholic' (64%) or 'mostly Catholic' (20%) areas. This experience may partly explain why they are less happy with residential mixing than they are with working alongside other groups. Nonetheless, there are considerable variations in attitudes depending on the group in question (Table 8). Living beside a member of a white group is generally more acceptable than a non-white group. However, among white groups, residence beside a Northern Irish Protestant is least favoured by Catholics. Indeed, Catholic churchgoers generally are almost as happy to have a Black neighbour. It is not insignificant that, despite their overall greater willingness for residential mixing, the young churchgoers actually prefer a Black neighbour to a Protestant. The limited experience of this group of living in mixed areas together with the security, both psychological and physical, that a segregated area provides especially in times of communal tension, may account for their reticence. The importance of security may also explain the fact that resistance is highest among the working class, the group which has been most exposed to negative experiences during the Troubles and which is most residentially segregated today.

Table 8. Attitudes to mixing as neighbours

		Per cent happy to have as neighbour					
		Southern Irish	English	N.I. Prot.	Black	Indian	Chinese
Sex :	Male	89	79	71	67	62	63
	Female	88	81	73	66	63	63
Age :	18 - 24	97	93	88	93	85	87
	65 or over	79	67	59	46	44	44
Orthodoxy :	High	84	73	63	58	54	54
	Low	92	88	85	77	73	75
Education :	Primary	80	69	57	53	49	49
	University	96	94	91	83	79	66
Occupation :	Unskilled	79	72	58	60	57	57
	Prof/Managerial	94	90	88	77	74	74
Total Population		**88**	**80**	**72**	**66**	**62**	**63**

Whether or not religious views colour these attitudes is uncertain. Whilst highly orthodox Catholics are more likely to be among those unhappy to have a neighbour who is not a Northern Irish Catholic this may be a factor of age rather than theology, given the large number of older churchgoers among the highly orthodox. Even then, two-thirds of highly orthodox churchgoers showed a willingness to live next-door to a Northern Irish Protestant.

In a further question, attitudes to future residential behaviour were also probed. Churchgoers were asked to indicate which kind of neighbourhood they would prefer to live in now. An 'all Catholic' area was preferred by 35% with a further 20% opting for an area which was 'mostly Catholic'. Over half of the Catholic population then, given the choice, would prefer to maintain residentially separate communities.

Marriage

This tendency for separation is also apparent in the choice of a marriage partner. Endogamous relationships are favoured. As Table 9 shows, only a quarter of Catholics indicated a willingness to marry a Northern Irish Protestant. These people were younger (59% under 45 years old), university educated (31%), in professional/managerial occupations (42%) and were less likely to be highly orthodox.

Table 9. Attitudes to mixing by marriage

		Per cent happy to marry					
		Southern Irish	English	N.I. Prot.	Black	Indian	Chinese
Sex:	Male	83	60	28	34	31	30
	Female	78	56	25	24	17	17
Age:	18 - 24	94	83	62	69	45	46
	65 or over	69	42	10	10	9	9
Orthodoxy:	High	74	46	12	17	15	14
	Low	87	72	51	44	36	35
Education:	Primary	72	43	10	14	13	12
	University	88	74	46	38	30	30
Occupation:	Unskilled	77	46	24	26	22	22
	Prof/Managerial	85	69	39	32	27	26
Total Population		80	57	26	28	23	22

Those over 55 and those whose formal education stopped at primary level were more resistant to mixing even across greater social distances. Their unhappiness about living next door to or working with Northern Irish Protestants is clear, although Catholics in general are willing to accept these less intimate relationships. It can be concluded, then, that age and education (see Figure 15) are the main contributing factors that differentiate between those who would and would not agree to mixing with Protestants.

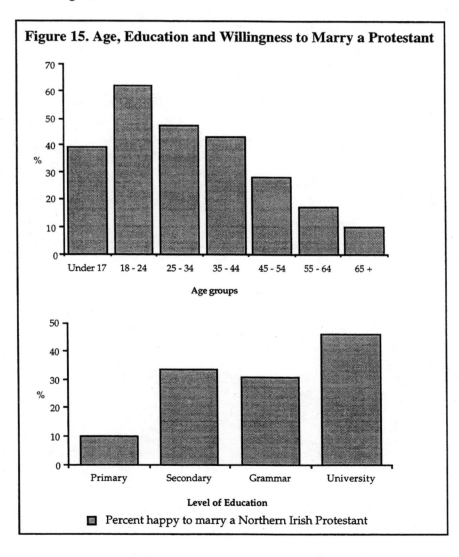

Figure 15. Age, Education and Willingness to Marry a Protestant

It must be noted, nonetheless, that the traditional Catholic Church expectation has been that Catholics marry Catholics. As might be expected, then, there was a strong negative correlation between attitudes to the importance of marrying a fellow Catholic and willingness to marry a Protestant. In line with this, a significant proportion of Catholic churchgoers (40%) believe it is 'extremely important' for them to marry another Catholic and they are, therefore, not at all positively disposed to marrying a Protestant. Attitudes varied, however, depending on the specific Protestant denomination in question. Almost two-thirds of Catholics (and 80% of over 65 years olds) said they would not be happy to marry a person from any Protestant denomination. However, for the third who would do so, the most favoured denominations were Church of Ireland followed by Presbyterian and Methodist. Once again those most open to intermarriage were the under 25s and the third level educated.

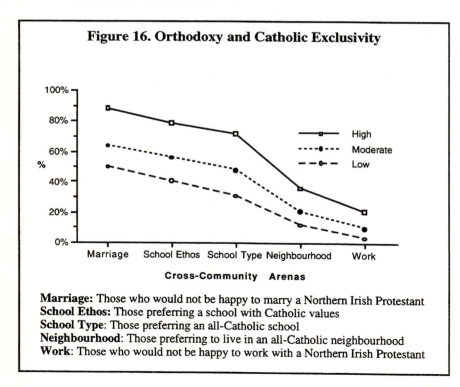

Figure 16. Orthodoxy and Catholic Exclusivity

Marriage: Those who would not be happy to marry a Northern Irish Protestant
School Ethos: Those preferring a school with Catholic values
School Type: Those preferring an all-Catholic school
Neighbourhood: Those preferring to live in an all-Catholic neighbourhood
Work: Those who would not be happy to work with a Northern Irish Protestant

As for marrying someone from outside Northern Ireland, non-white groups were no more popular than Northern Irish Protestants, except for Blacks. In this respect, as Table 9 has already shown, males display less exclusivity for, consistently, a higher proportion of them stated that they would be willing to marry a person of another ethnic group in the case of an Indian or Chinese partner.

Finally, there may be links between differences in social openness and levels of religious commitment. As Figure 16 shows, Catholics of low and moderate orthodoxy are more willing to mix with Northern Irish Protestants in all contexts than those of high orthodoxy.

Education
A further area of inter-group mixing was examined separately. Schools, according to some observers of Northern Ireland affairs, hold the key to better community relations, in that they can have a strong influence on social values. They conclude that mixed schooling of Protestant and Catholic children is the panacea. Others, however, argue for the maintenance of denominational schooling on the grounds that schools contribute in an essential way to religious formation (Murray, 1985; Loughran, 1987; McMackin, 1993; Moffat, 1993). Our churchgoers were asked, therefore, about their preferences for the education of their children, firstly, in terms of the numerical balance of Catholics and Protestants in the school and, secondly, in terms of the religious ethos of the school. They were also asked about their attitudes to joint school projects between children in Catholic and Protestant schools.

More than half of Catholic churchgoers (57%) indicated an unequivocal preference for a school for their children in which all pupils were Catholic. On the other hand, fewer than three in ten stated a preference for one with equal numbers of Protestant and Catholic pupils, and this was slightly more likely to be the choice of the younger age groups.

This general preference for separate schooling was further strengthened when preferred religious values within the school were considered; two-thirds of Catholic churchgoers would prefer a school with

Catholic values and only one third a mixed/interdenominational school. Indeed, 56% underlined that it would be wrong not to send a child to a Catholic school. It should be noted, nonetheless, that a contingent attitude was adopted by four out of ten who felt that it would depend on the circumstances.

A very wide range of the Catholic church-going population opted for Catholic schools, among whom only a very slight tendency towards the older and primary educated groups was evident. Not unexpectedly, those whose Catholic commitment was strongest in terms of orthodoxy (high and moderate) and frequency of church attendance were the strongest supporters. In contrast, the majority of low orthodox respondents (54%) were more likely to favour schools with both Catholic and Protestant religious values. The importance attached to Catholic schools by churchgoers does not mean, however, that they are against mixing in other aspects of education; a massive 96% favoured encouraging Protestant and Catholic children to join together in school projects.

These attitudes to education suggest an openness to mixing, but not at the expense of Catholic values and identity. They also reflect, when considered alongside attitudes to residential mixing and to marriage, the universal tendency of being more comfortable with 'one's own', especially in times of tension.

A range of attitudes to cross-community mixing, then, parallels the demographic characteristics already observed and points to the significance of religious mindset. In the religious arena, there is almost universal approval of ecumenism. Full church unity, the option most frequently favoured by the older more orthodox churchgoers, is as well supported as religious and social co-operation. Attendance at joint services presents little ideological problem even though opportunity may be restricted in certain social environments. Mixing in more social contexts, however, depends on the level of intimacy involved and on age, education and theological stance. Exclusivity is highest in marriage but decreases in the residental arena and again in the workplace for all groups. As for schooling, while there is almost universal support for Catholic and Protestant children working together on joint projects, a strong voice across a wide range of churchgoers indicates that this will not be at the expense of Catholic values and identity in the Catholic school.

Identity and Political Outlook

The social and religious mixing already discussed is intimately bound up with conceptions of belonging. In turn, identity typically finds expression in the political arena through a variety of ideological commitments. Accordingly we now turn to an elucidation of connections between Catholic identities and political outlooks.

Identity

The terms in which people describe both the place to which they belong and their national feelings can be instructive about their identity. This is even more likely where there is not a consensus among the inhabitants on political allegiance. We will now move to explore these sentiments and the political partisanship to which they lead.

Place Identity

Just under a half of Catholic churchgoers in Belfast refer to the place in which they live by using its political title of Northern Ireland (48%). The vast majority of the other half use descriptions that operate within the context of Ireland as a whole; 19% call it Ireland, 14% the North of Ireland, 11% the North and 5% the Six Counties (see Figure 17). Only an insignificant 1% refer to it as Ulster, yet this is the appellation employed almost universally by the media.

Whilst, in general, age makes little difference to the term used, it is significant that the under 17s have the highest proportion of any group referring to their place of residence as 'Ireland'. On the other hand, education levels distinguish place identity more clearly. Although at every educational level the highest proportion of churchgoers favour the politically accurate term, Northern Ireland, the trend is strongest for those with a university education (57%) and weakest among those with a primary education (45%).

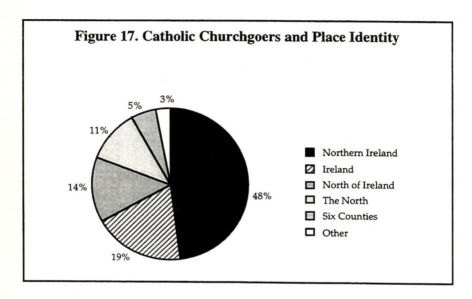

Figure 17. Catholic Churchgoers and Place Identity

- Northern Ireland
- Ireland
- North of Ireland
- The North
- Six Counties
- Other

Inevitably, there are also some attitude differences associated with differences in place identity. Those from 'Northern Ireland' were most open-minded when it came to social mixing, 30% of them being happy to marry a Protestant compared to 23% of the 'Ireland' group. They were more likely to be involved in cross-community organisations and to support the Alliance Party (11% compared to 2%). Those whose sense of place was described within an 'Ireland' framework were most likely to call themselves 'Irish' (95%) and to consider the political future as being within a United Ireland (89% as compared to 61% of those saying 'Northern Ireland'). They were also more likely to give support to Sinn Fein (23% compared to 5%).

National Identity
In a state where an understanding of the fundamental conflicts over national identity is imperative, our respondents were also asked to indicate how they would describe themselves. The overwhelming majority of Catholic churchgoers (96%) consider that their identity lies in some form of Irishness. As Figure 18 shows, almost seven out of ten regard

themselves as unequivocally Irish in contrast to just over two out of ten who claim to be Northern Irish. Further small percentages (3% each) describe themselves as Ulster Irish or British Irish. What is abundantly clear, however, is that no more than 2% consider themselves to be British.

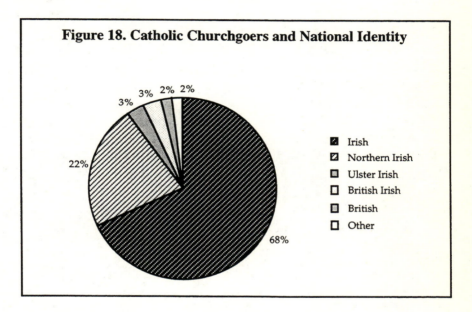

Figure 18. Catholic Churchgoers and National Identity

Those calling themselves 'Irish', as might be expected, are representative of the Catholic church-going population in general, in their age, sex, education, occupational background and employment status. They also reflect the entire theological spectrum. However, the greater Irish consciousness of the younger Catholics is worth noting; more than three-quarters of the under 35s describe themselves—in no uncertain terms—in this way.

The 'Northern Irish', conversely, are under-represented among the under 35s. They are more likely than are the 'Irish' to be female and to be university educated. On religious matters, however, they are no different, but they are slightly more open to all forms of cross-community mixing. This carries through to education so that, as Table 10 shows, they are less likely to be in favour of Catholic schools than the 'Irish', either in terms of numerical balance or of ethos.

In political terms Catholic churchgoers of both national identities feel strongly, and in equal proportions, that the SDLP most closely represents their views (see Table 10). However, it is the 'Northern Irish' who display more support for the Alliance Party and less support for Sinn Fein. As for the political future of Northern Ireland, the great majority of the 'Irish' are in agreement that it lies in becoming united with the rest of Ireland (83%). In contrast, a much smaller proportion of the 'Northern Irish' interpret the future in these terms (53%). Instead, a quarter of them favour remaining part of the U.K., an option cited by only 6% of the 'Irish'. As for an independent Northern Ireland as an option, only a small minority of both groups have a preference for such a future and then it is the 'Northern Irish' (15%) who are more likely than the 'Irish' (6%) to give it their support. These issues will later be examined in more detail.

Table 10. Comparison of Irish and Northern Irish identities

		'Irish'	'Northern Irish'	Overall
School Preference:	100% Catholic pupils	62%	48%	57%
	Catholic religious values	70%	57%	65%
Closest Political Party:	SDLP	71%	70%	69%
	Alliance	3%	12%	7%
	Sinn Fein	16%	4%	12%
Political Future:	United Ireland	83%	53%	72%
	Union with U.K.	6%	25%	13%
	Independence	6%	15%	9%

Political Partisanship
Whilst national identity and place identity are expressions of deep seated feelings about self determination, political partisanship may be of more immediate and practical relevance. As has already been

observed, Catholic churchgoers are strongly in agreement that the SDLP (69%) comes closest to expressing their political views. Only 12% aligned themselves with Sinn Fein and even fewer with the views of the Alliance Party (7%). Fewer still, only three people, stated a preference for a Unionist Party.

Given their numerical domination among churchgoers, then, SDLP supporters are a cross-section of the Catholic church-going population in their general characteristics. As Table 11 shows, however, Sinn Fein has a more youthful support structure and is more likely to be favoured by manual workers, especially the unskilled. The higher occupational class structure of Alliance supporters, on the other hand, reflects a higher educational profile in that they attract more university educated Catholics proportionately than any other party.

Table 11. Political Party Affiliation of Different Catholic Categories

		SDLP	Sinn Fein	Alliance
Age:	Under 45	61%	16%	7%
	45 or over	73%	10%	7%
Education:	Primary	74%	13%	3%
	University	69%	8%	12%
Occupation:	Professional/Managerial	70%	6%	14%
	Unskilled	63%	15%	6%

These better educated Alliance supporters are also more likely to be of moderate to low orthodoxy in relation to church teachings, as compared to those of higher orthodoxy who are more likely to support the SDLP or Sinn Fein. The SDLP also attracts the most frequent and traditional churchgoers and those most likely to conform to church rules. In contrast, Sinn Fein gets the largest support from those convinced that individual conscience is the most important guide to living a Christian life. Nonetheless, Sinn Fein are less likely than SDLP supporters to have attended an ecumenical service or to be involved in cross-community organisations. This tardiness in such matters may be linked to area of residence and the very high proportion (80%) living in 'all Catholic' areas which afford little opportunity for convenient mixing. Given that their personal experience of such mixing may be more limited, Sinn Fein supporters exhibit more open-mindedness when it comes to mixing with other ethnic groups than do SDLP supporters. The exception is in the case of mixing with English people, with whom Sinn Fein supporters are marginally more likely to want 'No Dealings' (7% compared to 2% of SDLP). Those who claim affinity with the Alliance Party are the most likely to be agreeable to residential mixing and intermarriage with all other ethnic groups. They are also more likely to favour religiously mixed schools in contrast to SDLP and Sinn Fein supporters who strongly favour Catholic schools (68% and 75% respectively).

The Irish identity of Sinn Fein supporters also surfaces in their place identity; they are more likely to identify with a place called 'Ireland.' On the other hand, SDLP and Alliance supporters are more likely to describe their place of residence as 'Northern Ireland' (51% and 75% respectively). Only Alliance supporters, however, carry this allegiance through in their national identity.

It must be remembered that the negative experiences of the last twenty-five years in Northern Ireland have not been equally borne by all Catholics and this may find expression in political outlook. Among Catholic churchgoers, one in five have experienced bomb damage on some scale to their houses and 14% have been forced through intimidation to move from their homes. Furthermore, death and injury have affected a substantial number; almost half of those surveyed have had a close friend, neighbour or relative killed or seriously injured. Indeed, over two-thirds of Sinn Fein churchgoers have had someone close to them killed or injured (see Table 12).

In contrast, fewer with Alliance Party views share the same history. The impact that such experiences have on attitudes is immeasurable, but they might be expected to affect particularly attitudes to mixing. The evidence suggests, however, that this is not necessarily the case. Rather, people who have experienced the Troubles, in any of the above ways, have average or above average positive scores when asked if they would marry, live next door to, or work with, a Northern Irish Protestant.

Table 12. Experiences of the Troubles

Experience	SDLP	Sinn Fein	Alliance
Home bomb-damaged	20%	25%	17%
Moved house due to intimidation	13%	20%	8%
Neighbour killed or injured	49%	65%	35%
Friend killed or injured	43%	67%	30%
Relative killed or injured	45%	67%	27%

Individual Catholic views about Protestants differ according to political party favoured. While Sinn Fein sympathizers were more likely than those of any other party to see a strongly united Protestant community, all churchgoers, regardless of party, were certain that Protestants get a fair deal today. But there was no such accord with respect to their view of the situation for Catholics. Whilst between a quarter and a third of SDLP supporters (27%) were satisfied that Catholics get a fair deal only a handful of Sinn Fein followers were in agreement (7%). In sharp contrast, two-thirds of Alliance supporters were satisfied, no doubt reflecting the personal experiences of this better educated group whose higher occupational structure may have given them social and economic advantages over the last quarter of a century in Northern Ireland.

Experiences may also colour attitudes to punishment. One third of Alliance Party supporters, for example, are in favour of capital punishment in some circumstances, in contrast to just over a quarter of SDLP supporters and only 14% of Sinn Fein adherents. But when it comes to security matters, however, Sinn Fein are least happy about the security situation being left to the security forces (89%). Among

Catholic churchgoers in general 62% take this same view, although what exactly they consider to be an alternative is unclear. These people are spread across all age groups but were a little better educated than those who agreed that only the security forces should handle it. Most of those in this latter group were over 45, attended church frequently and were highly orthodox in their attitudes to church teachings; they could be described as law and order types, comfortable with the order and certainty within which they had been brought up.

It is clear that there is no such thing as a monolithic Catholic identity. Whether expressed in terms of place or national feelings or reflected in political affiliation, identity is affected by age, education and class differences and by position on the orthodoxy scale. In general, however, Catholics are united, in being non-Ulster and non-British in identity and non-Unionist in politics.

Politics
And so to the future. Are Catholics a monolithic group when it comes to looking forward? Do they share the same views on major issues such as the root cause of the Troubles which need to be addressed and do they see religion and territory as inextricably linked?

Religion and Territory
There is certainly general accord among Catholic churchgoers in relation to the link between religion and territory. They overwhelmingly disagreed (80%) when asked if they thought that the Catholic faith could only flourish in a united Ireland. Of the 12% who saw such a territorial need more than half were over 65 and were educated to primary school level only. They may reflect earlier twentieth-century days when the 'Faith and Fatherland' concept had some currency.

Religion and Politics
There was less agreement on the role that religion plays in the Troubles. Whether the Troubles in Northern Ireland are mainly motivated by religion or by politics is a question which has exercised the minds of many analysts of the Northern Ireland situation over the

last 25 years. Varying degrees of importance have been attributed to religious factors by these commentators (Rose, 1971; Galliher and De Gregory, 1985; Wallis *et al.* 1986; Todd, 1987; Whyte, 1990; O'Connor, 1993). Some consider religion to be a basic causal factor while others deny its importance, favouring instead a political analysis.

As many as four out of ten of our churchgoers attributed the Troubles today mainly to religion rather than mainly to politics. Even allowing for the fact that we were sampling a conscientious and religiously motivated section of the Catholic population, such importance attached to religion has not always been recognised (Whyte, 1990). What then distinguishes this 'religion' group from the 'politics' group? Although the 'religion' group and the 'politics' group show some internal diversity, a pattern emerges which suggests that there are common characteristics which bind together members within each group.

The smaller 'religion' group is of higher average age, has a shorter formal education and has a tendency to come from manual backgrounds. Furthermore, it attracts those with the strongest religious convictions (45% of high orthodoxy), in contrast to the less orthodox churchgoers who are more likely to consider the Troubles to be mainly about politics (64%).

The evidence also suggests that they tend to have strict, less flexible codes of behaviour whether in regard to church affairs or to more secular social matters. Consider, for example, the reactions of the 'religion' group to ecclesiastical change; the introduction of women into roles traditionally held by men, such as eucharistic ministers, altar servers or indeed as ordained priests, consistently attracts less support from them. They adhere strongly to traditional views on other matters, such as the importance of a Catholic upbringing for children. Their own ecumenical experiences are more confined than those of the 'politics' group, as only 43% of them compared to 55% of the latter have actually attended a joint service of worship.

This greater concern with preserving enduring traditions also surfaces in varying attitudes towards societal arrangements designed to accommodate those with different views and backgrounds. For example, 'religion' respondents are among those Catholic churchgoers who are least likely to find civil divorce acceptable in any circumstances or to indicate a willingness to live in mixed areas. Consistently, too, they were 10-15% less likely than the 'politics' group to express a willingness to mix not only with Northern Irish Protestants but also with any other ethnic group. The political support of both groups, however, is most likely to go to the SDLP.

Political Frameworks
The majority of Catholic churchgoers (72%) across theological space see the long term future of Northern Ireland as being with the rest of Ireland. In order to get closer to an understanding of why this is so, churchgoers were asked to select from a number of possible reasons. There is little doubt where consensus lies since two-thirds of them highlighted that a united Ireland would give them the opportunity to express their Irish identity. Every other explanation warranted no more than 10% support (Table 13). For example, 7% suggested the more religious reason that Catholics would prefer to live in a Catholic

Table 13. Reasons why many Catholics want a United Ireland

Reasons	% of churchgoers
Because they could express their Irish identity	65
Because their standard of living would go up	8
Because they would prefer to live in a Catholic country	7
Because they would be a majority	5
Because they would gain a privileged position	5

country. These were a distinctive group as three-quarters were over 55, over half had only a primary education and two-thirds of them were highly committed to church teachings. Surprisingly, only one in ten of those who considered the Troubles to be about religion gave this 'religious' reason. There was no such consensus, however, in Catholic perceptions of why so many Protestants are opposed to a united Ireland. One in three suggest that it might be due to a Protestant wish to keep a privileged position. A slightly more educated group believe that Protestants fear the power that the Catholic Church might have in a united Ireland (24%). There were those, too, who felt that Protestants simply didn't want to be in a minority (14%) or that they were afraid of losing their British identity (13%). And what of those Catholic churchgoers in favour of political options other than a united Ireland? Thirteen percent were attracted to remaining as part of the U.K. and again they were scattered across all sections of Catholic churchgoers. In spite of this vision for the future the majority of these (60%) found that the SDLP came closest to representing their views.

Finally, just under one in ten Catholic churchgoers (9%) consider Independence for Northern Ireland as the favoured option. Closer scrutiny of their characteristics reveals that the majority of them are younger churchgoers (56% under 45), are more open to mixing with Protestants and other ethnic groups and are a little better educated on average than those with other outlooks for the future of Northern Ireland. Their higher occupational background suggests that Northern Ireland may have been kind to them.

There is a strong feeling, however, that Northern Ireland has been less than kind to Catholics in general. Only 27% of Catholic churchgoers agree that Catholics get a fair deal even today. Although these come from all age groups, they tend to be better educated (24% third level) and from non-manual backgrounds (61%). Their attitudes, then, may well be coloured by their personal experiences. Nonetheless, 65% of this group still believed that a person's religion matters in getting a good job in Northern Ireland.

Of the substantial body of Catholic churchgoers (73%) who considered that Catholics do not get a fair deal today there was likewise the almost universal (95%) belief that a person's religion matters in getting a good job. Such high proportions with these views on job opportunity are likely to be reflected in low levels of political faith in Northern Ireland. These attitudes are also likely to have repercussions for their perception of the position of Catholics in comparison to Protestants in

Northern Ireland. In this a united front is evident; a massive 96% of Catholic churchgoers agreed that Protestants get a fair deal these days. Among these, 87% were clear that religion matters in getting a good job and even the handful who were not so confident about Protestant opportunity still concluded that religion mattered.

This massive perception of the centrality of religion, especially in the workplace, may be a hangover of past mistrust. Nonetheless, it is clear that it is a fundamental issue that unifies the Catholic church-going population which may be divided on many other issues. It is essential, therefore, that it is addressed in terms of future arrangements for Northern Ireland. What must also be addressed is how to come to terms with the fact that Catholic churchgoers very strongly favour a political future where Northern Ireland is united with the rest of Ireland.

Conclusion : Diversity Or Unity?

The evidence gathered from our survey leads to the conclusion that Catholics, even churchgoers, do not form the strongly united community that is frequently purported to exist. Firstly, there are those who are highly committed churchgoers and those who are not, the latter a selective group which is younger and which is more likely to be unemployed. The absence from church of young people may reflect a more secularized era of socialization or a perception that the Church is irrelevant to their lives in the 1990s: whatever, the ideological gap between them and their churchgoing co-religionists appears to be widening and separate worldviews emerging. As for the unemployed, mindsets fashioned by the experience of three decades of socio-economic transformation and conflict, combined with perceptions of unrelieved inequality, are not compensated for by church attendance.

Among those who are churchgoers, any impression of solidarity is fractured by the range of theological convictions and attitudes on church affairs and moral and doctrinal teachings. Variation in age and in level of education contributes most significantly to understanding the diversity, not only of religious practice and belief, but also of attitude to moral, social and political matters. Indeed, on a very wide range of issues there is little to indicate internal coherence or consensus. However, when it comes to the matter of identity and to the constitutional future of Northern Ireland there is little evidence of disagreement; Catholics are united in being non-Ulster, non-British and non-Unionist.

Nonetheless, when considered overall, it must be concluded that the monolithism ascribed to Catholics is not borne out by the facts even among those who are churchgoers. Fewer than half of them believe—what has been shown to be a misconception in this research—that the Catholic community is strongly united. Of those Catholics who do believe this almost all finished their education at primary school and they are heavily concentrated in 'all Catholic' areas of Belfast. They contrast with the residents of 'mixed' areas who are highly likely to describe Catholics as being very divided. However, it is not insignificant that more than two thirds of all Catholic churchgoers are in agreement that the Protestant community is strongly united. Even if 'us' do not exhibit social solidarity there is a strong perception that it exists among 'them'.

III

Protestant Churchgoers

General Introduction

The cultural landscape of Belfast is punctuated by the artifacts of institutional religion. The occasional presence of Catholic churches, however, stands in marked contrast to the multiplicity of their Protestant counterparts. Everything from the grand cathedral to the humble mission hall represent the diverse expressions of Ulster Protestantism—a diversity equally evident on the church's page in the Saturday edition of the *Belfast Telegraph*. Our concern here, however, is not with the material structures or ecclesiastical architecture, but with the people whose lives are bound up, in varying degrees, with these religious spaces.

From the data we have gathered an overall picture quickly emerges of Protestant churchgoers in Belfast. Generally speaking they tend to be female (59%), over the age of 45 (73%), and to come from middle class backgrounds (64%). These characteristics are indicative of an important trend in religious life over the past decade. Comparison with our 1983 results indicates an ageing churchgoing population (Boal *et al.*, 1985). For whereas over sixty-fives comprised 24% of our 1983 sample, this figure has now risen to 40%. The fact that a large proportion of our current sample are women further illustrates this trend. Churchgoing is increasingly an activity practised by the elderly and by women. Of course there may well be denominational variation and we will examine this in due course.

In this chapter we seek to explore continuities and discontinuities in the attitudes of Protestant churchgoers in Belfast to a wide range of issues of contemporary importance. These include specifically religious questions of faith, belief and practice, as well as matters of wider societal concern to do with political life, public morality, cultural identity and cross-community relations.

Religious Belief and Practice
Because this is a survey of frequent church attenders it is not surprising that commitment to traditional doctrinal beliefs and the practices of personal piety remain at very high levels: 78% pray once a day, while 85% or more believe firmly in such standard doctrines as the Resurrection and the existence of the Devil and that the Bible is the Word of God. These expressions of 'orthodoxy', moreover, evidently extend considerably beyond the two-thirds who claim themselves to have had a conversion experience. Protestant churchgoers in Belfast— whether evangelical or not—are, by and large, conservative in their theological convictions. This does not mean, of course, that there are no significant differences in belief and practice—just under a half read the Bible once a day while 'speaking in tongues' is fully accepted by only 35%. But what is noticeable is that the strongest expressions of traditional doctrinal conviction are to be found amongst young people: biblical inerrancy is espoused by 78% of people under 24 years of age whereas for the over 65s it drops to 50%. By the same token younger people are more likely to adhere to the centrality of a conversion experience as crucial to genuine Christianity (82% of 17-24 year olds and 57% of the over 65s) and to claim that they have had such an experience themselves. These patterns that connect age with doctrinal conservatism also find expression in attitudes to women clergy, where the highest approval is to be found amongst the over 65s whilst lowest approval is displayed by the 25-34 age group. Overall, 64% expressed approval of women clergy, a view perhaps surprisingly shared almost equally by men and women. Apart from queries over the ordination of women, our churchgoers expressed a considerable degree of approval for women's participation in church organisations as church treasurers (87%), as missionaries (99%), and as Sunday School teachers (100%). For all that, a substantial majority (70%) preferred to hear the word 'man' rather than 'humankind' used in Scripture readings. Responses to this question, moreover, did not vary with gender. Churchgoing

women in Belfast, it seems, are no more enthusiastic about inclusive language than men. Indeed, as we shall subsequently see, it seems that gender is much less important than position on the theological spectrum, social class membership, or even party political preference in tracking attitudes to such women's issues.

Public and Private Morality
On issues of public and private morality considerable variation is evident among churchgoing Protestants. Consider first the question of Sunday Observance. Attitudes to this issue have remained remarkably constant over the past ten years, though if anything, contemporary churchgoers are a shade more conservative than a decade ago. Only one-fifth or less are prepared to engage in recreational activities, shopping, attending a sports event or going to the cinema on Sunday, though 50% read Sunday newspapers. Moral conservatism clearly remains at high levels and is further expressed in the fact that 70% favour the re-introduction of corporal punishment in schools and the re-institution of capital punishment in certain circumstances. Even more marked is our finding that 92% are convinced that 'courts let wrong-doers off too lightly nowadays.'

On issues of sexual morality the same moral conservatism is evident. Cohabitation before marriage and pre-marital sex are regarded as entirely unacceptable by two-thirds of churchgoers, while over 80% adopt the same moral stance over homosexual practice. Besides, whilst changes in sexual mores over time are generally regarded as stemming from the newer behavioural styles of young people, our data reveal that churchgoers under the age of 25 are, if anything, more likely to advocate traditional sexual moral standards than their middle-age counterparts. This attitudinal pattern regarding sexual mores may well reflect the fact that younger respondents are more likely to have conservative or evangelical religious convictions.

Although only 36% of regular Protestant churchgoers believe that abortion is wrong in all circumstances, this certainly does not imply that they hold a strongly pro-choice position. Save for circumstances in which the mother's life is at stake (84%), where pregnancy is the result of rape (66%) or an unborn child is likely to be severely physically handicapped (53%), our respondents adopt a broadly anti-abortion ethic. Moreover, this overall pro-life stance is equally advocated by both men and women; that is to say attitudes to abortion do not vary between the sexes. Age, however, *does* make a considerable difference especially over the issue of the risk of handicap: over sixty-fives are considerably more likely to allow abortion (61%) in such circumstances, than the under twenty-fours (29%). Whether this reflects the fact that over sixty-fives have more experience in the realities of family life and child-rearing or is a consequence of a greater awareness of pro-life issues among the younger generation of churchgoers remains unknown.

While regular churchgoers, it would seem, have remained generally immune to social change in attitudes to sexual morality and abortion, the same does not seem to be the case with divorce: 63% approve of divorce on the grounds of adultery, while 73% believe that it is legitimate when physical violence has occurred. Nevertheless, only 34% believe that the incompatibility of partners provided justification for divorce. These figures, moreover, conceal considerable diversity according to the age of the respondents. Under thirty-fives are more willing to accept divorce on the grounds of adultery (nearly 80%) than over sixty-fives (56%). Correspondingly, while one in five under the age of thirty-five believe that the incompatibility of partners provides reasonable justification for divorce, nearly two in five of the over sixty-fives take this view.

Social change also seems to have had a considerable influence on churchgoers' attitudes towards the circumstances in which they think it is acceptable for women to go out to work. The key circumstance in which churchgoers oppose women's employment is where they have children under school age. Only 40% find this acceptable. Surprisingly perhaps, the gender of respondents makes little difference, whereas, age is crucially significant. Only 18% of over sixty-fives approve of women going out to work when they have pre-school children, while this is true for around two-thirds of respondents under thirty-five. Further evidence for the significance of social change here is available from comparison with our 1983 survey.[1] At that stage, less than one in ten of the churchgoers attending those churches which we re-surveyed in 1993, approved of women working when they had pre-school age children; now, it is over four in ten.

Social and Political Affiliation
This strength of doctrinal conviction and religious practice that Protestant churchgoers display, should not be mistaken as indicative of a commonly held assumption that few Protestants are interested in cross-community religious interaction. Forty-four per cent claim to have attended an ecumenical service of worship and 47% favour religious and social co-operation between Protestants and Catholics. However, it must be noted that it is the over sixty-fives who are somewhat more likely to support such ventures: half of the over-65 age group compared to one-third of the 17-24 age group. On the other hand, actual involvement at a social level in cross-community organisations is strongest within the younger age cohorts. Also, we find that around 40% would like to live in an area with an equal mixing of Protestants and Catholics whilst a similar number claimed that they preferred children to be educated in a school with more or less equal numbers of Protestant and Catholics. Indeed, 91% supported cross-community school projects. Of course many continue to hold other convictions: 60% want their children schooled in an environment suffused with Protestant values, while only 14% indicated a preparedness to marry a Roman Catholic—a figure comparable to marrying members of such other ethnic groups as Blacks, Indians and Chinese.

Regardless of the substantial declared interest in cross-community links, when it comes to questions of the constitutional future of Northern Ireland there is little disagreement among churchgoing Protestants. Some 90% of our respondents expressed the conviction

---

1. There was a slight variation in the question between 1983 and 1993. Whereas, in 1983 the question asked about *married* women with children going out to work, in 1993 the question was about women with children going out to work.

that the long term political future of Northern Ireland should be as part of the United Kingdom. This strength of conviction, however, does not mean that churchgoing Protestants are united in their reasons for opposing a United Ireland: 32% oppose re-unification because they want to retain their British identity but even more (37%) say that Protestants oppose a United Ireland because of the fear of the Roman Catholic church. This suggests that more attention needs to be paid to questions of political motivation for, evidently, a unified constitutional stance may well be the product of diverse underlying aspirations.

On the question of perceived national identity, while churchgoing Protestants are certain they do not think of themselves as Irish (a mere 2%), they express a considerable ambivalence as to how they positively identify themselves; while 41% prefer to designate themselves as British, 36% want to emphasise the Ulster dimension of their identity (by describing themselves as either Ulstermen/women, or Ulster British), and 13% opt for Northern Irish. The strongest support for the use of this latter designation is to be found in the youngest age group of which over a quarter describe themselves as Northern Irish compared to 8% of the over 65 age group. So far as party political preference is concerned, 14% give their allegiance to the DUP, 21% to Alliance and 49% to Unionist. The youngest of our churchgoers are the most likely to favour the DUP (24% of the 17-24 age group compared to 12% of the 65 plus age group), though it should be noted that this age group is also the most likely to say that none of the political parties in Northern Ireland comes close to expressing their own viewpoint.

In our investigations thus far it is clear that there is very considerable attitudinal variation among Protestant churchgoers on a wide range of moral, social, and political issues. Analytically, it turns out that age matters a good deal more than gender in conditioning the pattern of responses we have discerned. In some cases this produces rather surprising results, such as younger churchgoers exhibiting more strict moral attitudes than their elders. And in this case, as elsewhere, other factors are evidently involved. Yet, if indeed there is considerable diversity, it would be mistaken to conclude that churchgoing Protestants are entirely disunited. Though they may belong to rather distinct religious subcultures with differing social attitudes, they nonetheless come together on major constitutional matters, perhaps revealing an unspoken conviction that Protestant diversity can only thrive within the protective fold of a distinct political entity.

The Denominational Landscape

Having undertaken a general reconnaissance of the Protestant churchgoing population in Belfast, it is now necessary to begin a series of explorations of intramural coalitions and clusters. Most obviously the variety of churchgoing Protestantism in Northern Ireland expresses itself through a very wide range of denominational affiliation. Judging by returns in the Census of Population (1991) in Belfast alone there are over 30 identifiable Protestant denominations. In our survey, responses were received from churchgoers of 13 denominations (see Table 14).

In order to render the body of data manageable, we have grouped the denominations identified in the table into seven categories. Beyond the three largest Protestant denominations—Church of Ireland, Presbyterian and Methodist—some scheme had to be devised whereby the remainder of the denominations could be organised into a coherent framework. The answer to Question 19 in Part 2 of the survey (see Appendix II) we believe helps provide a suitable basis for classification. This question asked respondents to specify 'Which other denomination do you think is closest in doctrine to your own?' Results from this question yield the schema provided in Figure 19.

Examining the clusters that emerged from this diagram we have analysed our data according to seven denominational coalitions, namely, Church of Ireland, Presbyterian, Methodist, Baptistic (incorporating Baptist, Brethren, and an Independent Evangelical church), Pentecostal/Charismatic, Other Presbyterian (incorporating the Free Presbyterian Church and the Evangelical Presbyterian Church) and Congregational. Reinforcement as to the appropriateness of this taxonomy is available both from in-depth interviews with clergy and from historical factors which connect certain traditions with each other.

For example, the category 'Other Presbyterian' encompasses two groups, which though self-consciously conservative Presbyterian in theological persuasion have historically seen their identity as distinct from mainstream Ulster Presbyterianism. Again, the Pentecostal/Charismatic coalition is united by the centrality accorded to certain supernatural manifestations of the gifts of the Spirit such as 'speaking in tongues.' The group labelled 'Baptistic' is consistently sceptical about such Pentecostal claims and has a fundamental commitment to adult Baptism.

Table 14. Denominations involved in the Belfast Churchgoers Survey 1993

Denomination	Number of Congregations
Church of Ireland	11
Presbyterian	11
Methodist	9
Baptist	7
Brethren	3
Evangelical Presbyterian	2
Free Presbyterian	4
Non- Subscribing Presbyterian	1
Congregational	2
Independent Evangelical Church	1
Moravian	1
Pentecostal	6
Non-Denominational Fellowship	1

**Figure 19. Denominational Clusters
showing perceived closest denominations**

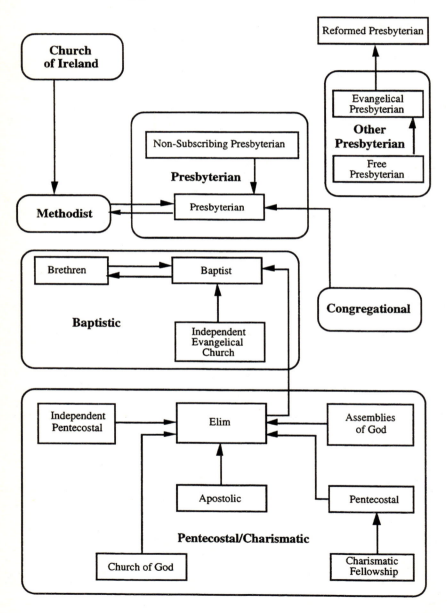

On matters of demography—age and gender—there is little significant difference across the denominational range. Having said this however, one or two discernible variations are apparent; the three largest denominations—Church of Ireland, Presbyterian and Methodist—have a comparatively older age profile than Baptistic, Pentecostal/Charismatic, Other Presbyterian and Congregational clusters. Indeed the Pentecostal/Charismatic grouping has much lower numbers in the 65+ age group (14%) compared to Presbyterian (47%) and Methodist (45%). Within this Pentecostal/Charismatic group, moreover, considerable variation is to be found; the overall 14% to which we have referred is actually derived from a mere 2% from a non-denominational Charismatic Fellowship and 18% from the other Pentecostalists. This, no doubt, arises from the character of the recent emergence of independent Fellowship churches which draw heavy support from young people. This young age profile is further reflected in patterns of educational attainment, where again, there is little variation denominationally. This means that those denominations with more conservative theological commitments are just as likely, contrary to conventional stereotypes, to have achieved the highest levels of educational attainment. The highest percentage for University attendance is to be found among the Baptistic groups (30%), compared to Church of Ireland (22%), Presbyterian (22%) and Methodist (13%). This is further reinforced by the proportion of Baptists who come from the professional class (24%), compared to Church of Ireland (13%), Presbyterian (18%) and Methodist (10%).

Faith and Commitment
Having characterised denominations by demographic structure, it is clearly important to ascertain how denominational affiliation conditions attitudes to a range of issues to do with faith and commitment. Our analysis, however, must not be taken to mean that denominations are purely self-contained entities; rather they are contingent affiliations of people, reflecting historical and contemporary circumstances.

Some denominations reveal much higher percentages of people who have not always belonged to that denomination. For example, while only 17% of Church of Ireland and 18% of Presbyterian attenders have ever been members of another denomination, 67% of Pentecostal/ Charismatics and 68% of Other Presbyterians have come from other traditions. No doubt in some cases these figures reflect factors to do with historical circumstances—for example, the Evangelical Presbyterian Church developed out of the Presbyterian Church in Ireland and therefore would be expected to have many older members who had changed their denomination. In other cases migration may reflect anything from marriage patterns to theological preference. Taken overall the three larger denominations (Church of Ireland, Presbyterian and Methodist) are decidedly more likely to be composed of people brought up in those denominations, whereas smaller groups like Baptist, Pentecostal and Other Presbyterian have considerable majorities who have transferred from other denominations (between 57% and 68%). Patterns of in-migration and out-migration are rather interesting. Figure 20 shows the ratio of those leaving denominations to those entering denominations for our 1993 survey; superimposed on this diagram are results from our earlier survey carried out in 1983 which shows the change over a ten year period.

Protestant denominations display remarkably high levels of doctrinal orthodoxy especially amongst the smaller denominations which, as we have just noted, have grown considerably in recent years. Belief in the Resurrection and 'that the Bible is the Word of God,' for example, attracts percentages in the mid-eighties and low nineties from Church of Ireland, Presbyterian and Methodist while for others it is almost invariably 100%. This does not mean that Protestant denominations display an undifferentiated doctrinal uniformity; on the question of 'speaking in tongues,' for example, this is believed firmly by around a third of Church of Ireland, Presbyterian, Methodist, Baptist and Congregational churchgoers. Amongst Other Presbyterians the figure drops to 16%, while for Pentecostal/Charismatic it soars to 95%. This latter contrast reveals considerable plurality between groups that might otherwise be typified as fundamentalist for they both share very high levels of commitment to one central element in the fundamentalist outlook—conversion (95%+), compared to Church of Ireland (41%) and Presbyterian (56%).

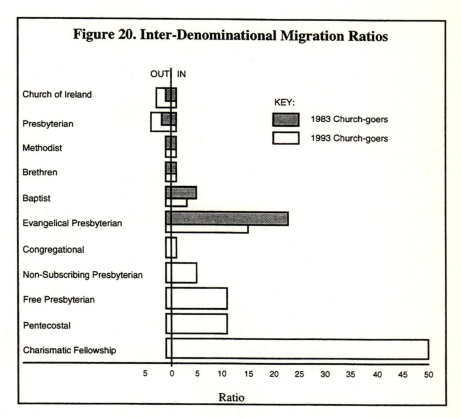

This depth of commitment to doctrine is further reflected in patterns of practice. Eighty per cent and more of respondents from the Baptistic, Pentecostal/Charismatic and Other Presbyterian denominational groups attend church at least twice on a Sunday compared with slightly more than a third for the three main denominations. Broadly similar results are also evident for daily prayer and Bible reading.

Given the patterns we have just discerned on traditional beliefs and practices, attitudes to the role of women in the church reveal an expected pattern. There is little difference between the denominations on the sending of women as church missionaries. But the question of the ordination of women produces considerable variation (see Figure 21). Women clergy are least approved of by Baptistic and Other Presbyterian groups (only around 5% strongly approve) but find considerable support from a majority of respondents within the main denominations. For all that, inclusive language is only supported by a minority of churchgoers, a majority preferring to hear 'man' rather than 'humankind' in Bible reading, with a particularly strong support for traditional modes of expression coming from smaller denominations.

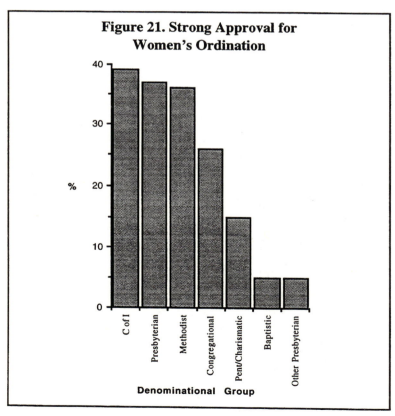

Although on many of the issues we have examined so far, the smaller denominations reveal substantial agreement, it is among these self same groups that a relatively stronger expression of individualism is to be found. Contrariwise, the three main denominations have fewer than one in five declaring a strong commitment to the individual, over against the institutional church. These patterns clearly reflect a firmer commitment to ecclesiastical tradition among the numerically stronger denominations; conversely the strongest expression of support for individualism is to be found among Other Presbyterians. This finding raises some intriguing questions when we note that support for the democratisation of certain religious practices (for example non-clerical administration of communion) is lowest among Evangelical Presbyterians and Free Presbyterians. At the other extreme are Baptistic churches with a strong commitment to lay involvement, with the three major denominations occupying a middle position. Thus it seems that the denominational group most committed to individualism in principle turns out to be the most committed to clericalism in practice.

The cleavage that is now emerging between the three larger denominations and Baptistic, Pentecostal/Charismatic, Other Presbyterian and Congregational traditions continues to characterise denominational responses to a variety of issues to do with inter-church relations. Attitudes to joint services with other Protestant denominations reveal that more than three-quarters of respondents from the larger denominations are 'happy to take part in a joint service of worship' with each other; rather less than half of them, however, find joint services with Brethren and Free Presbyterians congenial. Indeed, it is worthy of considerable note that respondents from these larger denominations are more willing to join with Roman Catholics than they are with these fundamentalist groups (see Figure 22).[2] Plainly the fractures within Protestantism on ecclesiastical matters run deep—deeper, perhaps, in

---

2. In Figures 21 and 22 percentages drop below one hundred for respondents' own denominations. This may be due to a perception that it was not necessary to complete the question for their own particular denomination.

some cases than the chasm of conventional Protestant-Catholic discourse. One reason for this pattern, of course, might be to do with perceived differential risk. The likelihood of losing members to the Catholic church is negligible; but, given the migratory transfers *within* Protestantism, risk of loss to these smaller denominational groupings is considerably higher. Besides, while Catholic liturgy can be accepted as the legitimate difference of the 'other,' the style of fundamentalist Protestantism might well be rather less comfortable to mainstream churchgoers.

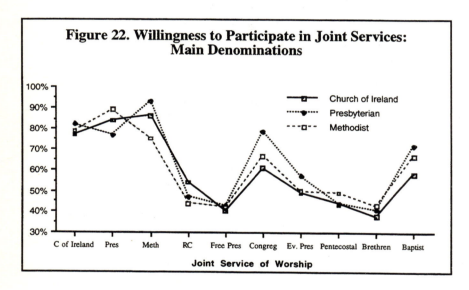

Correspondingly, smaller denominations are much more willing to join with other conservative evangelical groups, and overall find joint services with Presbyterian and Methodists more acceptable than Church of Ireland. Not surprisingly, rather less than one-quarter are willing to take part in joint acts of worship with Roman Catholics (see Figure 23). It is noticeable that Free Presbyterians are the least prepared of any group to participate in inter-denominational services, and particularly, are unwilling to join with the Roman Catholic church or with the three main Protestant Denominations.[3]

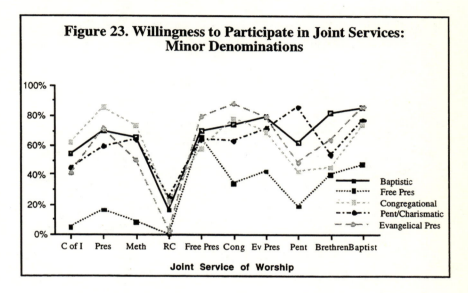

Expressing a willingness to be involved in joint Protestant and Roman Catholic services is one thing; actual participation in an ecumenical event is quite another. Our findings reveal that slightly over half our respondents from the main denominations have participated in such events, while for the smaller denominations this is the case for only one-quarter, with the number falling to 6% for Other Presbyterian.

Broadly similar alignments are also to be found in responses to questions to do with future relations between Protestant and Roman Catholic churches, as Table 15 shows. The smaller denominations are, generally speaking, unwilling to go beyond social co-operation, whereas larger denominations are rather more prepared to engage in religious and social inter-church relations. Church unity does not seem

---

3. Conversely when it comes to marrying across the divides, the main denominations are less prepared to welcome marriage with Free Presbyterians and Pentecostals than with other denominations.

to be particularly welcomed by any of the groups, though the Church of Ireland seem rather more inclined to aim for unity than the other larger denominations. It is particularly noticeable from this table that those expressing greatest interest in church unity come from the Pentecostal/Charismatic group. This might seem surprising given the

Table 15. Future Relations between Protestant and Catholic churches

Denomination	Unity	Religious and Social Co-operation	Social Co-operation	No Association
Church of Ireland	14%	54%	25%	6%
Presbyterian	9%	60%	28%	4%
Methodist	11%	57%	26%	5%
Baptistic	5%	19%	59%	17%
Pentecostal/Charismatic	21%	22%	40%	18%
Other Presbyterian	3%	3%	43%	49%
Congregational	16%	33%	39%	12%

solidly evangelical convictions they express. Two factors, however, may help explain this pattern. First, the advent of a series of Protestant/Catholic charismatic encounters has provided a forum for inter-denominational dialogue. Secondly, and perhaps more speculatively, it may be the case that some of those supporting unity within this group may do so on the assumption that it is on their own terms. Indeed there is additional evidence to suggest that this question could be interpreted in such a way—one Free Presbyterian respondent urged that church unity was to be welcomed 'when the Church of Rome is reconciled to the God of the Bible.'

Cross-Community Relations

Attitudes to ecumenical services of worship are only one (and indeed restricted) expression of cross-community interaction. Beyond such church-based activities, further attitudes to Protestant and Catholic linkages can be perceived in a variety of other arenas. Consider first the educational sphere. Apart from the Church of Ireland (48%), all the other denominational groupings reveal a majority of respondents who prefer to have their children educated in a school with exclusively Protestant values. Thus while the figures are 51% and 57% respectively for Methodist and Presbyterian, it rises to 69% for the Baptistic cluster, 80% for Congregational and 92% for the Other Presbyterians. Not surprisingly, the smallest support (less than 3%) for schools with shared Protestant and Catholic values comes from Other Presbyterians, compared with Methodist (47%), Church of Ireland (46%) and Presbyterian (39%). Support for such schools from Baptistic groups (22%) and Pentecostal/Charismatic traditions (25%) conceals some interesting variations. Take first the Baptistic denominations. Here, whilst one quarter of Baptists and Brethren give their support to schools with mixed religious values, only 3% from the Independent Evangelical Church adopts such a stance. Among Pentecostal/Charismatic chuchgoers there is also considerable variation. A full 50% from the Independent Charismatic Fellowship are supportive of such schools compared with 17% from other Pentecostal churches. Once again the monolithic application of labels like 'evangelical' or 'fundamentalist' to such denominations effectively obscures significant variations when it is assumed that such churchgoers inevitably adopt highly traditional attitudes to cross-community endeavours. The emergence of groups designating themselves as Evangelical Catholics further attests to the fluidity of ecumenical taxonomy.

Not surprisingly these findings are closely correlated with attitudes to the type of school to which Protestants prefer to send their children where again we see that those groups most in favour of a school with mixed religious ethos are also those most supportive of a school with equal numbers of Protestant and Catholic children. Figure 24 shows the pattern of response to school type ('All Protestant,' 'Mostly Protestant' and 'Equal Protestant and Catholic') from our seven denominational clusters.

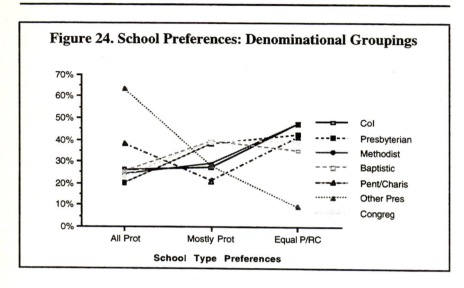

Figure 24. School Preferences: Denominational Groupings

Clearly there is considerable variety of opinion amongst regular churchgoers on this matter and this is nowhere so dramatically revealed as in the contrast between Free Presbyterian and Charismatic Fellowship responses to the question (see Figure 25). Yet again, monolithic stereotyping of evangelical Protestantism fails to do justice to the internal variety that is actually present.

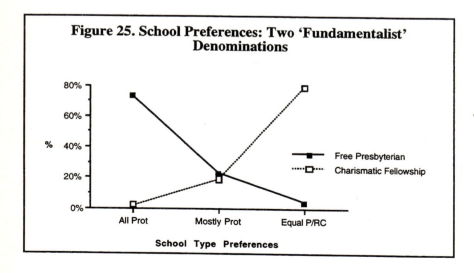

Figure 25. School Preferences: Two 'Fundamentalist' Denominations

Attitudes to the type of school to which churchgoers would prefer to send their children provide only one measure of social interaction across the communities. Views about mixed Protestant/Catholic marriage provide another indicator and in this case a much less open stance is discernible. Indeed, save for the Church of Ireland, Protestant churchgoers, it seems, are rather more willing to accept inter-'racial' marriage than Protestant/Catholic marriage (see Figure 26)—a pattern which is even more evident amongst the smaller denominations.

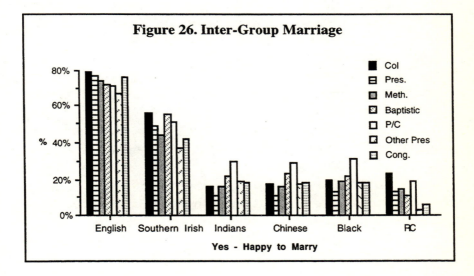

Noticeable also here is the comparatively lower standing of Southern Irish compared with English which may reflect either pro-British sentiments and/or anti-Catholic bias. By the same token the substantially higher response of Southern Irish compared to Roman Catholic indicates that some of our respondents evidently did not make the assumption that 'Southern Irish' always means 'Catholic'.

A third indicator of attitudes towards cross-community relations is to be found in questions to do with neighbourhood composition. Here, there is a comparatively greater openness to cross-community mixing, with around a half of Church of Ireland, Presbyterian, Methodist, Baptistic and Pentecostal/Charismatic respondents expressing a preference for living in a community with equal numbers of Protestants and Catholics. The one group where such support is conspicuously lower is Other Presbyterian where the figure is 15%.

Despite clear evidences of support for cross-community endeavours, a considerable expression of what might be termed Protestant alienation is clearly detectable. In attitudes to fairness in Northern Irish society an overwhelming majority of all denominations is convinced that 'Catholics generally get a fair deal.' By contrast a significant minority of between 20%-30% feel that Protestants do not get a fair deal; indeed in the case of Other Presbyterians a majority feel this way.

Political Identity

On a number of key issues to do with political identity, there is overwhelming agreement across the denominational divides. Thus, over 80% are convinced that 'Northern Ireland should remain part of the United Kingdom.'[4] Similar proportions agree that 'the security situation in Northern Ireland should be left entirely to the security forces.' At the same time the vast majority of all denominations feel that there is either no or very little understanding by 'people "across the water" ... why many Ulster Protestants want to maintain the Union with Great Britain.'

On the question of national identity a majority of all denominations wants to build in a strongly British component, by designating themselves British or to a lesser extent Ulster British. It is worth noting, however, that the strongest support for the designation Ulsterman/woman is forthcoming from the Other Presbyterian group, where 35% identify themselves by this label, compared with less than 20% from all other denominational groupings. These patterns find predictable expression in party political preference among churchgoers (see Figure 27). Beyond the broad-band of support for official Unionism, the DUP

---

4. The 20% remaining suggest other solutions to the Northern Ireland problem, such as Independence (4%-12%), a European Solution (around 1%), Devolution (around 1%) and Majority Rule (1%-2%). Figures advocating a United Ireland range from 0% to 7%.

derives proportionately greater support from the smaller denominations (and in particular 77% from Other Presbyterians), while Alliance attracts a quarter of Church of Ireland, Presbyterian and Methodist churchgoers.

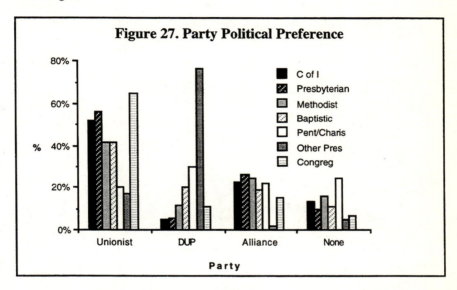

While Protestant churchgoers are evidently concerned to retain their British identity, when it comes to reasons why they feel that Protestants object to a United Ireland, fear of 'the power the Roman Catholic church would have in a United Ireland' was the most common answer. What is noticeable, however, is that while for the larger denominations the difference between this response and 'afraid of losing British identity' was only in the order of 2% to 3%, among the smaller groupings the gap widened to 15% for the Baptistic cluster and 43% for Other Presbyterians (see Figure 28).

If Protestant opposition to a United Ireland springs from an uneasiness about the loss of national or religious identity, it is highly significant to note that more than 75% of all denominations (except for Other Presbyterians—69%) believe that at some stage in the future, more than half the population of Northern Ireland will be Roman Catholic, with all the political and religious implications inherent in such circumstances. Indeed, around half of all Protestant denominations are assured that this demographic change will be effected in the next 20 years.[5] Such findings run directly counter to the political aspirations that the

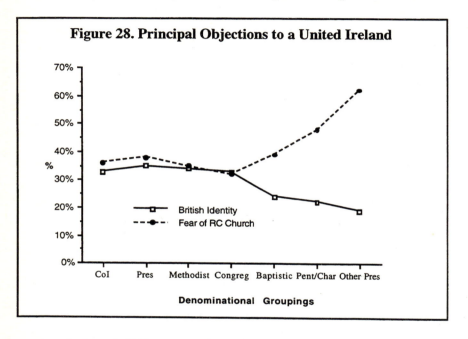

Figure 28. Principal Objections to a United Ireland

vast majority of all Protestant denominations (80-95%) share, namely, that Northern Ireland's long term political future should be to remain part of the United Kingdom. Do we here perhaps sense again a siege mentality amongst Protestants, who, whilst perceiving themselves likely to be outnumbered in the not-too-distant future, nevertheless remain overwhelmingly committed to a future within the United Kingdom? For all that, Protestant churchgoers have a sense that the Catholic community is relatively more united than their own (see Figure 29).

---

5. It is worth noting that in our 1983 survey a slightly larger proportion of churchgoers made the same prediction.

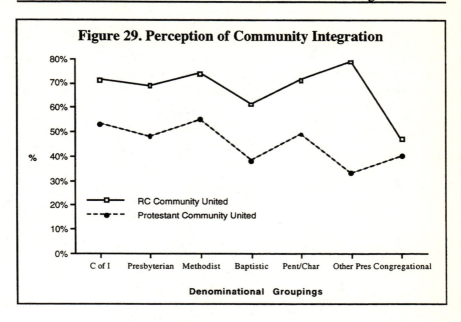

Figure 29. Perception of Community Integration

Given these expressions of both ecclesiastical and civic identity, it is also noteworthy that for a large minority of Protestant churchgoers their theological convictions are tied to Northern Ireland's geographical space. Between one-quarter and one-third of denominations (rising to almost a half of Other Presbyterians) expressed the view that the flourishing of the gospel depended upon the continuance of the protective shield of the state. By the same token, a large majority of churchgoing Protestants plainly do not see the future of their faith as directly dependent upon politico-geographical circumstances.

Private and Public Morality
Denominational affiliations also express themselves in varying measures of what might be called social and moral conservatism. Using responses to ethical questions concerning pre-marital sex, living together outside marriage, abortion and homosexual practice, it was possible to devise a scale of moral judgement from the strict (consisting of those who believed that all these practices were always wrong) to liberal

(consisting of those willing to accept the legitimacy of some of these practices), with a variety of intermediate positions.[6] As can be seen from Figure 30 a major divide exists between the larger denominations where less than 30% can be described as strict moralists and the smaller denominations where the figure rises to 40% and more; within this second grouping moreover, the Pentecostals/Charismatics and Other Presbyterians emerge as even more widely adopting a strict moral stance. Conversely, liberal attitudes are scarcely discernible amongst the smaller denominations, whereas the larger denominations have between 14-24%.

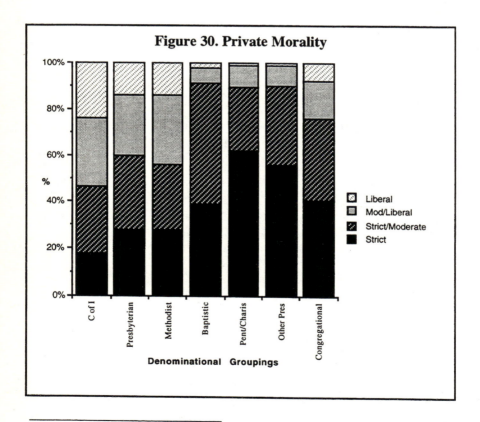

---

6. See Appendix IV for private and public morality scales.

A similar exercise was carried out to produce a corresponding scale for social attitudes. Here, attitudes towards caning in schools, leniency in courts and capital punishment were used to distinguish social conservatives (who strongly agreed with all these propositions) from liberals (who disagreed or strongly disagreed). As can be seen from Figure 31, denominational patterns of public morality are rather less dramatic than patterns of private morality. Nonetheless it is noticeable that the Other Presbyterians adopt the most conservative position (52%) followed by Pentecostals/Charismatics (35%).

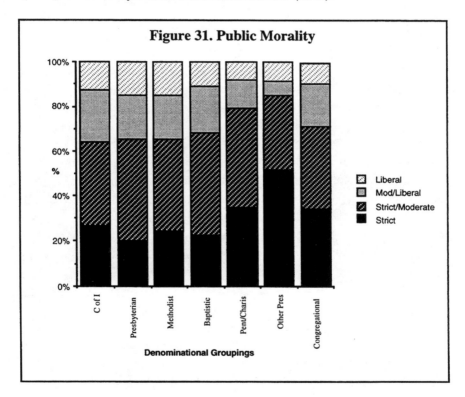

Speculating on the basis of these few variables is undoubtedly a risky exercise. Yet, there would seem to be some grounds for suggesting that Protestant churchgoers, particularly those from the smaller denominations, are inclined to take up stronger positions on issues to do with private morality than with public morality.

Protestant churchgoing, then, comes in a wide variety of denominational styles. In an attempt to seek for some coherence within this ecclesiastical heterogeneity, we devised and subsequently deployed a seven-fold denominational taxonomy in our analysis. Throughout, a remarkable diversity of attitude, belief, and behaviour, varying by denominational affiliation, has manifested itself. Denominational allegiance, to put it another way, matters a good deal in accounting for cultural variation within churchgoing Protestantism. Indeed some denominations are more hesitant to join with certain smaller Protestant groups than with Roman Catholics even in religious ventures. Nevertheless, despite this variety, we have detected a significant divergence in stance between the three larger denominations and their smaller counterparts. On such issues as ecumenism, objections to a united Ireland, cross community connections, and both public and private morality, churchgoers from the Church of Ireland, Presbyterian and Methodist traditions display somewhat different attitudes from fellow Protestants in the other denominational groupings. As we shall presently see, a good deal of this diversity is explicable by reference to the spectrum of theological conviction displayed across the denominational landscape. And yet we have been alerted to the dangers inherent in stereotyping particular groups, for example as 'fundamentalist', when the assumption is that they necessarily would display identical social and political attitudes. For it turns out that within theologically conservative denominations widely differing positions on matters—such as schooling—may be adopted, positions which standard stereotyping fails to detect. It is appropriate, therefore, to turn now to the theological spectrum to ascertain its significance in conditioning the beliefs and behaviour of churchgoing Protestants.

The Theological Spectrum

While denominational affiliation evidently makes a significant difference, as we have just seen, to a wide range of attitudes among Belfast churchgoers, other studies both here and elsewhere have pointed to the even greater significance of theological convictions, lying on a spectrum from fundamentalist to liberal (Martin, 1982). If indeed this is the case, it becomes important to determine whether a person adopts a theologically conservative or liberal set of beliefs. The validity of this assertion was confirmed in our earlier 1983 investigation of Protestant churchgoers in Belfast (see Boal, Campbell and Livingstone, 1985). Accordingly, we now turn to an examination of the influence of theological convictions in conditioning the attitudes of contemporary churchgoers. Our respondents fall into three relatively distinct categories of belief. The Conservatives[7] are those who retain both a strong commitment to the central importance of a conversion experience and a firm belief in Biblical inerrancy. Liberals adopt neither of these commitments,[8] while the group we have designated Liberal-Conservative espouse one or other of them. Taking all our Protestant churchgoers, we find that 50% occupy the Conservative category, with 25% Liberal and a further one quarter fall into the middle Liberal-Conservative group. The numerical predominance of Conservatives that these figures reveal further confirms our 1983 findings; indeed if

---

7. We choose to characterise our respondents as conservatives because the labels fundamentalist and evangelical carry a range of associations that are not necessarily implied in our designation.
8. See questions 10 and 12 in Part II of the Protestant Questionnaire. *Conservatives* are those who indicated on question 10 that '*Only a conversion experience of Jesus Christ as personal Saviour makes you a Christian*' and on question 12 that '*What is written in the Bible is the Word of God and is completely without error.*' To qualify as a *Liberal* an individual ticked a box other than the *conversion* one on question 10 and other than the '*completely without error*' category on question 12. In other words our liberals are neither conversionist nor inerrantist in any sense. This must not be taken to mean however that no liberals report that they themselves have undergone a personal conversion experience. Indeed 22% record that they *have* experienced such a 'turning point'. Evidently such people despite their own experience do not want to make conversion a *sine qua non* of genuine Christian commitment. The *Liberal/Conservatives* can be *either* conversionist *or* inerrantist and are therefore intermediate between the first two groups.

anything there has been a marginal increase in the proportion of those of Conservative persuasion. Thus when we examine the seventeen churches common to both the 1983 and the 1993 surveys we find a 3% increase in Conservatives and a corresponding 3% decline in Liberals. If nothing else these findings indicate that theological conservatism is continuing to thrive and that theories assuming the decline of either fundamentalism or evangelicalism with the progress of industrial modernism must be seriously questioned.

It must be stressed that this theological spectrum does not map directly onto denominational affiliation (see Table 16); almost every denomination encompasses churchgoers who occupy different points on this theological spectrum.

Table 16. Theological Composition of Denominational Clusters

	Conservative %	Liberal-Conservative %	Liberal %
Church of Ireland	27	28	45
Presbyterian	38	29	33
Methodist	43	35	23
Congregational	79	17	4
Baptistic	83	15	1
Pentecostal/Charismatic	87	12	0.4
Other Presbyterian	94	6	0

Nevertheless, certain denominations are more heavily concentrated in one of the categories while others are spread across the three groups. Thus Baptistic, Pentecostal/Charismatic and Other Presbyterian denominational clusters are overwhelmingly Conservative (between 83% and 94%), with no more than one per cent falling into the Liberal camp. Among the larger denominations all three points on the scale are strongly represented, although in the case of the Church of Ireland the largest percentage is Liberal (45%), whereas for Presbyterian and Methodist the largest percentages—Conservative—are 38% and 43% respectively. Plainly, as we have already said, the theological spectrum from Conservative to Liberal cross cuts denominational affiliation in highly significant ways.

The Demographic Dimension
While gender does not make any significant difference to whether our respondents are Conservative, Liberal-Conservative or Liberal, age turns out to be highly significant. Those in the younger age cohorts are overwhelmingly Conservative in their theological convictions compared with those in the older age groups. Of those between 18-24 years of age 76% are Conservative compared with only 10% who are Liberal. For the over 65's by contrast the proportions change to 41% and 32% respectively. Generally speaking the percentage of Conservatives declines as one moves through the different age bands (see Figure 32). Having said this it must be noted that, because the churchgoing population is an ageing one, the majority of both Conservatives and Liberals are of course in the older age brackets.

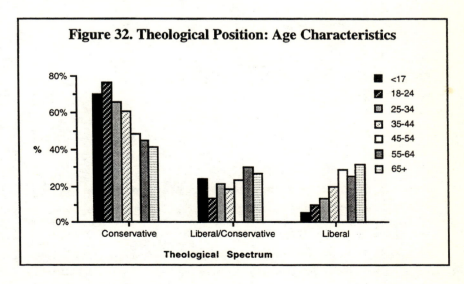
Figure 32. Theological Position: Age Characteristics

Compared with our data from the 1983 Belfast Churchgoers Survey we find that for the 17 churches investigated in both surveys, younger people are even more likely now to be Conservative in their theological opinions. For those in the 25-34 age group for example, 72% fall into the Conservative category compared with 54% a decade ago. However, for those aged 45 years and over there has been little change between the two time periods and indeed churchgoers in these age bands are just as likely to espouse a Liberal viewpoint as a Conservative one.

So far as educational attainment is concerned Liberals are somewhat more likely to have achieved higher levels of education (28% having had a university education compared to 18% of Conservatives) while Conservatives are much more likely to have left school after primary or secondary-intermediate schooling (60% compared with 35% for Liberals).[9] Of course, because of the numerical predominance of Conservatives we must note that of those churchgoers who have had a University education 45% are Conservative compared to 34% Liberal. These findings also have a direct bearing on the matter of social class. Conservatives and Liberals each attract around 40% of churchgoers from the professional classes, whereas over three-quarters of the semi-skilled and unskilled manual classes are Conservative compared with less than 10% for Liberals.

Insofar as one can generalise about the theological spectrum in demographic terms, it is particularly striking that churchgoers who are at the more youthful end of the age spectrum and those who are members of the working class show a clear tendency to occupy the more conservative side of the theological range. Two different, but related, processes would seem to contribute to this pattern. Conservative success in maintaining a more youthful age profile may well reflect more efficient *retention* strategies due to the activities of a variety of denominational and interdenominational evangelical organisations. The predominance of conservatives among working class churchgoers, on the other hand,

---

9. McEwan and Robinson (1994) have recently examined links between education and evangelicalism.

is, perhaps, a product of *residualisation*—namely the residential legacy of selective out-migration of people in the earlier phases of the life cycle from areas where there is a predominance of more evangelical churches. There is, of course, something of an irony in these findings: the groups which are least likely to be church attenders overall, are most likely—if they do attend church—to adopt theologically conservative values.

Religious Belief and Practice

So far as matters of religious belief and practice are concerned there are dramatic differences between Conservatives and Liberals which have been overlooked too frequently in analyses of social life in Northern Ireland. We should recall of course, that it is on the basis of beliefs concerning conversion and the Bible that we have discriminated between Conservatives, Liberal-Conservatives and Liberals. But differences in doctrinal beliefs extend considerably beyond these. Such cardinal doctrines as the Resurrection and the Bible as the Word of God are unambiguously espoused by all Conservatives compared with between two-thirds and a quarter of all Liberals. On other matters however the gap between these groups widens significantly. All Conservatives remain firm in their belief in the existence of Heaven, Hell and the Devil while among Liberals these are only firmly believed by 63%, 39% and 52% respectively. On all these indicators it must be noted that the Liberal-Conservatives stand much closer to Conservatives than to Liberals. This reinforces the idea that, theologically at least, our Liberal-Conservatives are indeed Conservatives with some Liberal tendencies rather than Liberals with Conservative tendencies. The high degree of doctrinal unanimity amongst Conservatives is not however universal. Less than half firmly believe in the phenomenon of 'speaking in tongues,' a figure that falls to one in ten amongst Liberals. There are significant differences in religious practice as well. Consider for example church attendance; whereas only 14% of our Liberal churchgoers go to church twice on a Sunday the figure rises to 74% for Conservatives. When we add to this the fact that 64% of Conservatives return to their churches at least once a week (many twice a week) to participate in other mid-week services compared with 12% of Liberals, the significance of these church spaces in the weekly routine of social life for Conservative believers is evidently of considerable proportions. Besides, the fact that 50% of Conservatives and 31% of Liberals are also involved in church based recreational activities lends further support to this assertion.

This behaviour is further reflected in a variety of practices connected with personal piety such as daily prayer and Bible reading, and family devotions. In all of these Conservatives are around four times more likely to regularly engage in such activities than those of Liberal outlook. Given the fact that 67% of Conservatives report reading the Bible once a day, it is worth pausing to note that 75% believe 'every passage in the Bible should be taken literally except where the Bible itself indicates otherwise'. At first glance, this may not seem surprising, since Conservatives have been designated in this report as those who believe in the inerrancy of the Bible. And yet it is clear that literalism and inerrantism do not map directly onto one another; for a fifth of Conservatives, even while accepting Biblical infallibility, reject the claim that the Bible must always be read in a literalist fashion. Contrary to popular opinion Conservatives may be inerrantist but not necessarily literalist, though many are. For all that, Conservatives remain loathe to adopt versions of the Bible using inclusive language. Some nine out of every ten Conservatives prefer versions of the Bible which retain the term 'man' rather than adopting the more inclusive 'humankind'. By contrast a majority of Liberals (54%) favour the use of the latter expression. Given these attitudes, it is not surprising that Liberals are considerably more approving of women preaching than Conservatives (88% to 60%), and are very decidedly more likely to approve of women's ordination (87% to 41%) (see Figure 33).

On these women's issues it is noticeable that, in contrast to their attitudes to a variety of doctrinal matters, Liberal-Conservatives are much closer to the Liberal viewpoint than that of the Conservatives. For example, while only 18% of Liberal-Conservatives and 10% of Liberals disapprove of women ministers, 51% of Conservatives oppose women's ordination. Plainly this issue is highly divisive; by contrast, greater lay participation in church services draws similar rates of approval from all three groups, as does the widely held commitment to the assertion that it is more important to remain loyal to one's own convictions than to one's own church.

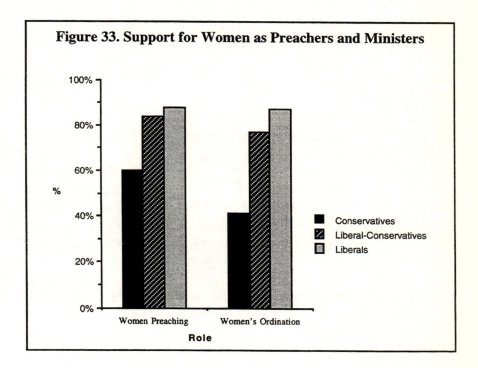

Figure 33. Support for Women as Preachers and Ministers

Shifting attitudes to Sunday observance represent a further aspect of social change. On this issue major differences are observed between Conservative, Liberal-Conservative and Liberal groups. Whereas only 12% of Conservatives are willing to 'attend a sports event on Sunday' the figure rises to 25% for Liberal-Conservative and 52% of Liberals. Comparable differences were also recorded for Sunday shopping—9%, 24% and 37% respectively. Certainly internal differentiation among churchgoers on this issue is plain; but equally notable is the persistence of a relatively strong Sunday observance ethic overall. Having said this, there have also been changes in Sunday behaviour among churchgoers over the past decade. Whereas in 1983 only 11% of Conservatives reported a willingness to buy a Sunday newspaper, by 1993 this figure had risen to 29%. In this same time period the figures for Liberal-Conservatives moved from 40% to 58% and for Liberals from 65% to 88%. A similar liberalising of attitude also surfaces in attitudes to watching television on Sundays. In 1983 42% of Conservatives gave their approval to Sunday TV viewing; by 1993 it was 60%. Again comparable figures for Liberal-Conservatives and Liberals show a shift from 70% to 88%, and 87% to 98% respectively. Taken overall it seems that contemporary Conservatives display Sunday attitudes comparable to those of Liberal-Conservatives ten years ago, with Liberal-Conservatives themselves now adopting stances that characterised the Liberals of a decade ago.

Overall, then, on matters to do with religious faith and ecclesiastical practice, position on the theological spectrum is of very considerable importance in conditioning the attitudes of churchgoers. Indeed there is evidence to suggest that the Liberal to Conservative range is of even greater significance than denominational affiliation in the production and reproduction of doctrinal conviction and in the regulation of church and everyday experience. At the same time we are not suggesting that these categories are themselves sufficient to account for all attitudinal variation. For example there are substantial minorities within each of the Liberal, Conservative and Liberal-Conservative groups who do not adopt the same outlook on particular issues. These interpretative categories, in other words, do not denote monolithic entities. Nevertheless, clearly there is strong evidence to support the view that theological conviction is of very considerable importance in the shaping of churchgoing Protestantism.

Cross Community
Profound differences in attitudes to cross community relations are also apparent among churchgoing Protestants. Dealing first with the more purely religious aspect of this issue we find that Liberals (64%) are decidedly more likely than Conservatives (27%) to have participated in an ecumenical service of worship. This gap widens even more dramat-

ically when we turn from actual participation to *attitudes* to joint services of worship with Catholics, for while 19% of Conservatives are happy to participate in such ventures, this is true for 71% of Liberals (see Figure 34). Not surprisingly, very few Conservatives—30%—are supportive of greater social and religious co-operation between

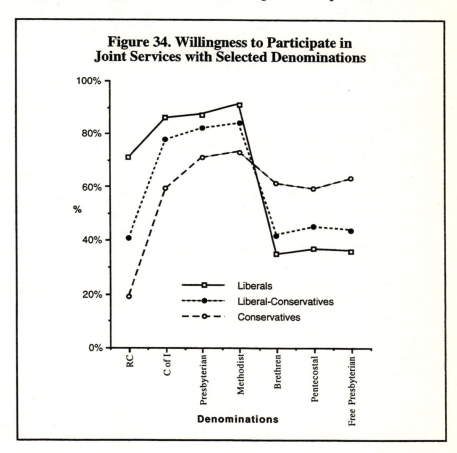

Protestant and Catholic churches, while 70% of Liberals are in favour of such objectives. There are of course other important dimensions to the issues of ecumenism that need to be registered. Primarily very few

churchgoing Protestants of any theological stripe express much interest in church unity (around one in ten).[10] Having said this however, Liberals (as we have seen) are enthusiastic about church services with Catholics (71%); this stands in marked contrast with such groups as Pentecostals (37%), Free Presbyterians (36%) and Brethren (35%). It is also noticeable that on almost every ecumenical issue the Liberal-Conservatives occupy an intermediate position.

Broadly similar attitudes also manifest themselves on the issue of mixed marriage. Taken overall there is an overwhelming opposition to Protestant-Catholic marriage, although predictably this is strongest among Conservatives—a mere 7% indicate a willingness to marry a Catholic compared to 28% of Liberals. Beyond this, a majority of Conservatives are willing to take a marriage partner from the range of Protestant denominations. By contrast, Liberals seem to be much more selective in the Protestant denominations from which they would happily choose a marriage partner; over 90% are favourably disposed to Presbyterian, Church of Ireland and Methodist, whereas for such denominations as Brethren, Pentecostal and Free Presbyterian the number is closer to one in four—a figure even smaller than for Catholics. All these values of course must be interpreted in the light of the finding that whereas only 20% of Conservatives were willing to marry a non-Christian (as they define it), this is true for 50% of Liberals.

Attitudes to mixed marriage are likely to have an impact on views about schooling. Not surprisingly, three-quarters of Conservatives prefer to have their children educated in a school with exclusively Protestant values and therefore want to send their children to either an all Protestant or mostly Protestant school. Correspondingly, only around one in five want a shared Protestant-Catholic ethos for their children's education compared with three in five Liberals. Once again

---

10. Some of the conservatives who expressed support for church unity might well have done so on the understanding that such re-unification could take place on their own terms. As we have already noted, one Free Presbyterian respondent stated church unity was to be welcomed 'when the Church of Rome is reconciled to the God of the Bible.'

the Liberal-Conservatives tend to occupy an intermediate position, though on the question of ethos they seem somewhat closer to the Conservative outlook. The same basic pattern of response also comes into attitudes towards neighbourhoods where respondents 'would like to live'. Conservatives are much more inclined to favour an all Protestant neighbourhood—21%—compared to 6% of Liberals. And overall as many of them prefer an all or mostly Protestant neighbourhood as favour an all or mostly Protestant school. But it must be noted that the tendency toward religious exclusivity is expressed with less strong conviction in neighbourhood preference than in school type preference.

Attitudes to mixed marriage, school ethos, school type, neighbourhood preference and work environment form a spectrum of views concerning aspects of cross-community interaction. The differences between Conservatives, Liberal-Conservatives and Liberals are recorded below on Figure 35. It can be seen that whereas the extent of

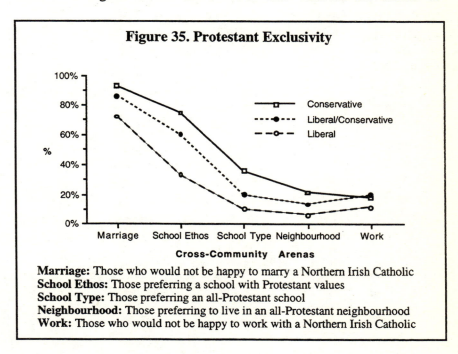

Figure 35. Protestant Exclusivity

Marriage: Those who would not be happy to marry a Northern Irish Catholic
School Ethos: Those preferring a school with Protestant values
School Type: Those preferring an all-Protestant school
Neighbourhood: Those preferring to live in an all-Protestant neighbourhood
Work: Those who would not be happy to work with a Northern Irish Catholic

Protestant exclusivity varies between the groups, the attitudinal pattern is remarkably consistent. Protestant exclusivity seems in every case to be more important for Conservatives than for either of the other two groups. This finding may help explain the fact that Liberals (by and large) identify with people of their own social class regardless of religion, while for Conservatives the opposite is the case. To put it another way, Conservatives are more likely than Liberals to think in terms of religion rather than class.

Public and Private Morality
Given the very considerable disparities that we have just identified among churchgoers on matters of religious belief and practice, the question arises as to whether these attitudes permeate other aspects of social life. Here we consider a number of moral issues ranging from public disciplinary procedures and institutions in society to matters of private morality in general and sexual mores in particular.

Turning first to the public arena and its most extreme expression of judgement—capital punishment—we find that a majority of Protestant churchgoers of all theological opinions would support its reintroduction, with the strongest supporting expression stemming from the Conservatives (Conservative, 75%; Liberal-Conservative, 68%; Liberal, 61%). The depth of concern over this issue that is recorded by Conservatives also comes through in their feelings that 'the courts let wrong-doers off too lightly' and that corporal punishment in schools should be brought back.[11] Nevertheless, this should not obscure the overwhelming agreement across the spectrum that is voiced concerning the judicial system; nine out of every ten churchgoers, across the theological range, are convinced that the courts are too lenient these days.

The differences here expressed between Conservatives and Liberals substantially widens when it comes to matters of divorce. Whether on the grounds of violence, mental cruelty, desertion, incompatibility or

---

11. In both cases there are 20% more conservatives than liberals who *strongly* agree with the propositions.

irretrievable breakdown, Liberals are in every case at least 25% more likely (and in some cases nearly 50% more likely) to countenance divorce (see Table 17). Liberals (and Liberal-Conservatives who, on this issue, tend to stand a little closer to the Liberal stance), evidently, are a good deal more willing to accept divorce than Conservatives. What is notable, however, is that despite this, Liberals are rather less likely to find adultery a legitimate cause for divorce. Sixty-seven per cent of Conservatives declare that divorce is legitimate in the case of adultery, whereas the figure for Liberals is 59%. Clearly the issue of sexual fidelity remains a salient component of the Conservative psyche and is, correspondingly, less prominent within the Liberal mindset, at least compared with other divorce-related circumstances.

Table 17. Grounds for Divorce

	Conservative %	Liberal-Conservative %	Liberal %
Violence	58	77	86
Mental Cruelty	53	70	80
Desertion	43	61	77
Incompatibility	18	37	55
Breakdown	30	57	78
Adultery	67	64	59

The cleavage between Liberal and Conservative moral stances, as revealed in attitudes to divorce, is even more accentuated when it comes to the question of abortion. To be sure, there is an overwhelmingly anti-abortion ethic shared by churchgoers across the theological spectrum in the sense that there is practically no support for the view that abortion is always, or even generally, morally acceptable. Having said that, the strongest opposition to abortion is forthcoming from Conservative churchgoers, 53% of whom declare that it is 'always wrong', compared with 25% of Liberal Conservatives, and 11% of Liberals. Correspondingly the greatest sense of equivocation is expressed by Liberals; 62% of them inform us that the morality of abortion is circumstantial, compared with 24% of Conservatives.

Although the strong anti-abortion sentiment that is expressed by Conservatives is entirely predictable, there is evidence to suggest that we find here an initial 'gut reaction' which, on further reflection, is actually rather more modulated in certain circumstances. For while 53% tell us that abortion is 'always wrong', only 15% insist (in replying to a separate question) that there are no circumstances whatsoever in which abortion should be legally available; moreover, 77% of them believe that abortion *is* acceptable when 'it is the only way to save the mother's life.'[12] In other circumstances—such as rape, the possibility of physical handicap, or when the mother-to-be is too young to assume parental responsibilities—Liberals are consistently more prepared to countenance abortion; indeed in each case the difference is of the order of 40%.

On matters of morality, the differences between Conservatives and Liberals are at their sharpest on questions of sexual behaviour. An overwhelming percentage of Conservatives thus find sex before marriage, cohabitation, and homosexual practices to be always wrong—88%, 85% and 94% respectively; for Liberals these figures drop to 31%, 28% and 56%. These figures clearly reveal substantial disparity in judgements about sexual morality, though the difference is a little less marked on the question of homosexuality.

In our comparison between Conservatives and Liberals on matters to do with public and private morality, we have discerned an increasing divergence of viewpoint as we move from questions about discipline in

---

12. When we identify the 53% of conservatives who say that 'abortion is always wrong,' we find that only 27% of them, when provided with a range of possible circumstances, confirm their initial reply by saying that abortion should not be available in any circumstances; and again, 66% (of the 53%) *are* prepared to have abortion legally available when it is the only way to save the mother's life.

society, through divorce and abortion, to sexual morality. This pattern is displayed in Figure 36 where Conservative and Liberal attitudes on key issues are mapped.

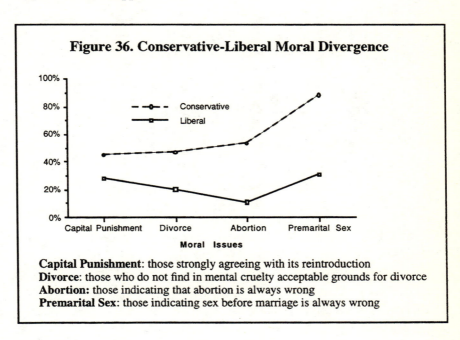

Figure 36. Conservative-Liberal Moral Divergence

Capital Punishment: those strongly agreeing with its reintroduction
Divorce: those who do not find in mental cruelty acceptable grounds for divorce
Abortion: those indicating that abortion is always wrong
Premarital Sex: those indicating sex before marriage is always wrong

Political Persuasion

Despite all the divergences between Conservatives and Liberals that we have identified in the religious, moral, and cultural spheres, when it comes to issues of politics and identity in Northern Ireland there is remarkably little variation in attitude. Of course this is not to say that there is *no* difference of outlook. Consider, for example, our findings on the question of which political party comes closest to respondents' current views. Overall there is a broad band of support across the theological spectrum for the Unionist Party; beyond that, Liberals are more inclined towards the Alliance Party and Conservatives towards the Democratic Unionist Party (see Figure 37).

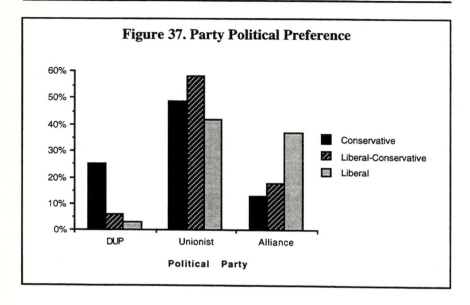

Figure 37. Party Political Preference

The only other political matter on which much divergence of opinion surfaces is in attitudes towards the Orange Order. The strongest expression of support is forthcoming from those of Conservative opinion—65%, with the figures falling to 62% for Liberal-Conservatives and 50% for Liberals. In some ways this is a little surprising given the traditional antipathy to the Orange Order from certain 'fundamentalist' denominations. However, we now find that the Orange Order attracts approval from nearly half of Brethren and Baptist churchgoers.

On other political issues, however, very little difference is to be found across the theological spectrum. Consider, for example, answers to the question as to why Protestants object to a united Ireland. On this issue similar patterns emerge across the theological groups. To be sure, Protestants overall differ on just what the objection is: for many it is a fear of the role that the Catholic Church would play; for others it is to do with losing British identity. But the key finding, at this point, is that these responses are *not* differentiated by theological conviction. The same is also true of the mirror-image question, namely, why Catholics in Northern Ireland want a united Ireland. Again some feel it is because

Catholics would prefer to live in a Catholic country; others mention the opportunity it would afford of expressing Irish identity; a few indicate that it is because Catholics would be a majority. These responses, however, are again *not* distinguished by theological commitment. And finally, the same is true of opinions as to how united both the Protestant and Catholic communities are. Over two thirds of each theological grouping felt that the Catholic community was strongly united; in terms of perceived Protestant unity the proportion falls to around 50%.

This lack of disagreement on political issues is nowhere more clearly revealed than in the constitutional question, where around 9 out of 10 insist that the long-term political future of Northern Ireland should be within the United Kingdom. Given the remarkable diversity of opinion that Conservatives, Liberal-Conservatives and Liberals espouse on so many moral and social issues, this unanimity may well seem surprising. What it clearly *does* reveal is that religious identity does not map on to political identity in any direct way (see Figure 38).

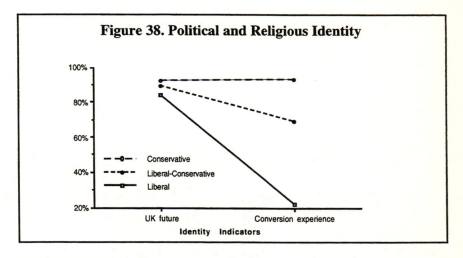

Theological conviction, it seems, has little bearing on political identity. By contrast, when we examine one key indicator of *religious* identity—the experience of conversion—the differences across the theological spectrum are immense; 93% of Conservatives report a born-again experience, compared with 69% of Liberal Conservatives and 22% of Liberals. The unanimity of political identity stands in marked contrast to the diverse expressions of religious identity. It seems as though the only way in which Protestants feel that they can maintain their religious and cultural pluralism is within a political monolith.

Even though Protestant churchgoers are most obviously discriminated by denomination, there is strong evidence for claiming that position on the theological spectrum taps an even deeper set of roots from which religious identity springs. Positioning on this scale, moreover, is not directly mappable on to denominational affiliation. Certainly some of the smaller denominations have much larger proportions of conservatives than others; but conservatives are to be found throughout the entire denominational range. On more purely ecclesiastical matters the influence of the theological spectrum is marked; but it also extends beyond this sphere to condition attitudes towards cross-community connections and public morality. If indeed the conservative-liberal polarity is as central to religious identity as our findings would seem to indicate, then the analysis of Protestant churchgoers using classifications that depend on census-type variables—like denomination—will persistently fail to come to grips with the complexities and contested character of the Protestant mind-set.

The Social Class Arena

While Protestant churchgoers are evidently distinguished by denominational affiliation and by their position on the theological spectrum, they are also characterised by social class.[13] It is therefore important to

---

13. The social classes we have identified are: Professional-Managerial [P-M]; Skilled Non-Manual [SNM]; Skilled Manual [SM]; and Semiskilled and Unskilled Manual [S-USM]. When we use the designation middle class we refer to Professional-Managerial and Skilled Non-Manual in combination; working class refers to the combination of Skilled Manual and Semiskilled and Unskilled Manual. The acronyms are used only in the

consider how social class impinges on the attitudes of churchgoers to religious, moral, political and social issues. First, however, we need to make some observations on the social class characteristics of our churchgoing population (see Figure 39). As we previously noted, regular churchgoing in Belfast is largely a middle class phenomenon.

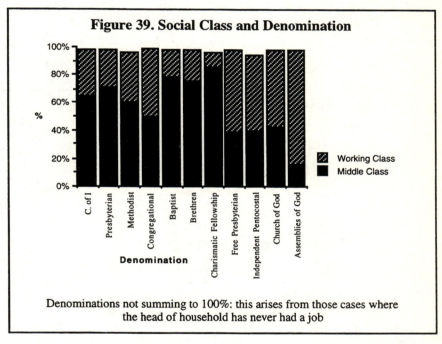

Figure 39. Social Class and Denomination

Denominations not summing to 100%: this arises from those cases where the head of household has never had a job

However, this is by no means a uniform pattern across the various Protestant denominations. The most middle class denominations, namely those with 50% or more attenders coming from a professional-managerial background, are Brethren, Baptist and an independent charismatic fellowship. The Presbyterian Church follows closely and is the most middle class of the three largest denominations with 46% coming from a middle class background. Working class church

---

figures. Each respondent's social class is established through the occupational categorisation of his/her 'head of household.'

attendance, by contrast, is more typical of a variety of Pentecostal churches and the Free Presbyterian Church.

There is also a distinctive social class pattern among Conservatives, Liberal-Conservatives, and Liberals on the theological spectrum. This, of course, is not unrelated to denominational profiles since some denominations are composed of a much larger proportion of Conservatives than others (see Table 16, page 96). The pattern of social class membership across the theological spectrum is portrayed in Figure 40.

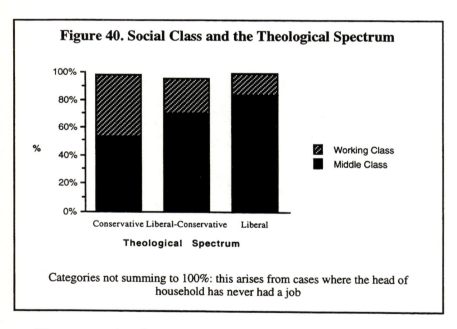

Figure 40. Social Class and the Theological Spectrum

Categories not summing to 100%: this arises from cases where the head of household has never had a job

There are also interesting connections between social class characteristics and the age and sex profiles of our churchgoing population. As we have already reported, regular churchgoers, taken overall, are somewhat more likely to belong to higher age groups and to be female. But what is particularly noticeable is that this pattern is class-differentiated. For example, whereas 31% of churchgoers from semi- and unskilled manual backgrounds are male, 69% are female. When we compare this with those from professional/managerial backgrounds the gender imbalance virtually disappears, namely, 48% are males and 52% are females. Clearly this shows that men who come from working class backgrounds are much less likely to be regular churchgoers than their middle class counterparts. These findings, however, should be considered in conjunction with age patterns—50% of churchgoers with a semi- and unskilled manual background are over the age of 65, compared with 33% from professional/managerial occupations. Given the gender imbalance, this pattern is to be expected. This means that those churches with a substantially working class constituency are likely to have a marked predominance of older women. No doubt this reflects the character of working class popular culture. The long history of working class defection from institutional religion, together with a sense that religion is only for the elderly and the women, would produce precisely the pattern we have discerned.

Social class membership also seems to have an important bearing on churchgoers' perceptions of inter-generational change in social position. Respondents were asked to identify the social class character of their current home background and of the home background in which they grew up. The greatest sense of upward social mobility was expressed by those with professional-managerial occupations. Only 44% of these identified their early home background as professional-managerial, whereas 93% perceived their current position as professional-managerial. This clearly reveals a quite remarkable sense of upward social mobility among members of this social group. By contrast, 76% of semi- and unskilled manual respondents identified their current home background as falling into this social category; 68% told us that this was their early home background, and 21% perceived that they had been brought up in skilled manual households. This, if anything, shows a perception among members of this social group of a sense of downward social mobility.

Taken overall, while Protestant churchgoing is a middle-class activity in the main, it is clear that class characteristics are not unrelated either to denominational affiliation, or to positioning on the theological spectrum.

Religious Observance

Having examined the class characteristics of regular Belfast churchgoers, we turn now to consider the salience of social class position in a variety of behavioural and attitudinal phenomena. Let us first examine a range of religious beliefs and practices. When we turn to frequency of church attendance, daily prayer, and Bible reading, it is noticeable that those from the more working class occupational backgrounds display somewhat higher levels of religious observance (see Figure 41).

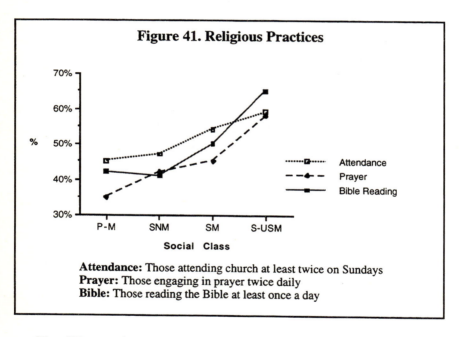

Figure 41. Religious Practices

Attendance: Those attending church at least twice on Sundays
Prayer: Those engaging in prayer twice daily
Bible: Those reading the Bible at least once a day

The diligence in religious observance and devotion displayed by the more working class component of our churchgoing population may also be reflected in the strongly conversionist stance that they adopt. Whereas 56% of those from a professional/managerial background believe in the centrality of a conversion experience, for semi- and unskilled manual churchgoers the figure rises to 83%. Taken overall, it seems as though those from a more working class background display a noticeable level of dedication in matters of religious belief and practice.

On the surface this seems to militate against the long-held view that the working class has undergone a long history of secularisation in British society, displayed in defection from institutional religion. What our findings indicate is that while this picture remains true at the general level, it is evident that those working class people who *do* remain within the church are particularly committed to the religious life. For example, compared with the upper middle class components of the churchgoing population, churchgoers from semi- and unskilled manual backgrounds seem relatively more committed to their church than to their own convictions. Whereas only 14% of the former put loyalty to their church above loyalty to their own opinions, this figure rises to 46% for the latter group. Besides this there is evidence that working class churchgoers are more likely than their middle class counterparts to hold on to traditional values and conservative beliefs.

Consider, for example, attitudes towards the ordination of women. While the differences here are not dramatic, there is a clear sense that respondents from semi- and unskilled manual background (most of whom are women) are rather less happy about having a female minister (54%) than those from professional-managerial households (66%). Much more conspicuous are the differences in attitude and experience to cross-community and ecumenical matters. Across the occupational spectrum from middle class to working class we observe a marked decline in the proportion of those who have attended a Protestant-Catholic religious service of worship (see Figure 42).

It might well be the case, of course, that those from more working class backgrounds have less opportunity to participate in an ecumenical service given the social geography of religious segregation in Belfast. However, when we examine *attitudes* to joint services with Catholics even in principle, we discover a much greater opposition among working class respondents. Whereas 55% of regular churchgoers from professional/managerial backgrounds would be happy to participate in such services, the figure drops to 15% among those from semi- and unskilled manual backgrounds. Indeed among those working class respondents who have never had the experience of participating in such a service, 95% indicate that they would not wish to avail themselves of such an opportunity even if it were available. Clearly ecumenical ventures are considerably less welcome among working class churchgoers.

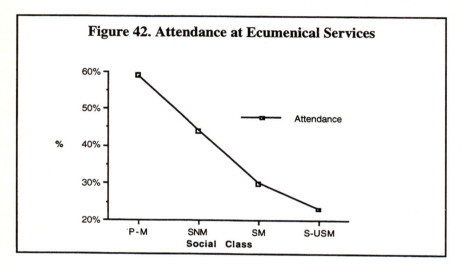

Figure 42. Attendance at Ecumenical Services

The same general tendency is also evident in feelings about other aspects of relations between Protestant and Catholic churches. Certainly the idea of church unity is attractive to very few regular churchgoers. Increased social cooperation is welcomed by around a third of our respondents irrespective of class; however when it comes to combining religious and social interaction there is a steady decline in support across the class spectrum, from 56% in the professional/managerial group to 34% among the semi- and unskilled manual.

Cross-Community

Having examined the different attitudes to inter-church connections according to social class, it is appropriate to turn now to less narrowly religious dimensions of cross-community relations. Of undoubted importance are the different residential arenas within which individuals are both physically and socially placed. Churchgoers, of course, are located in these diverse neighbourhood spaces in which the processes of social reproduction are effected; but they occupy a variety of religious spaces too—spaces no less significant in the dynamics of socialisation—by virtue of their participation in a range of church environments. In the Belfast context, religious composition of neighbourhoods is widely regarded as of crucial importance. The type of neighbourhood in which churchgoers find themselves and the character of the areas in which they would prefer to live, given the opportunity, turn out to be strikingly different across the social class strata. Figure 43 displays the pattern of neighbourhood composition, both present and preferred, for the different occupational groupings: the low levels of segregation among the professional/managerial groups stand in marked contrast to the much more highly segregated experience and preference of working class churchgoers.

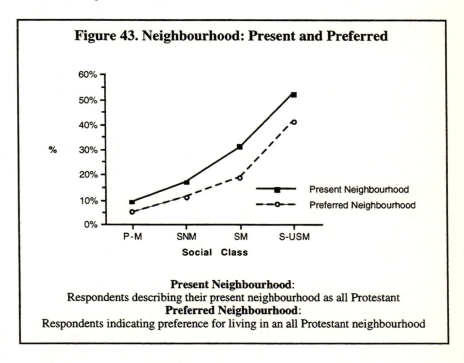

Figure 43. Neighbourhood: Present and Preferred

Present Neighbourhood:
Respondents describing their present neighbourhood as all Protestant
Preferred Neighbourhood:
Respondents indicating preference for living in an all Protestant neighbourhood

It would be mistaken, however, to interpret this as evidence for a complete lack of interest in greater residential mixing on the working class end of the occupational spectrum. If we examine the experience and degree of preference for neighbourhoods with equal numbers of Protestants and Catholics, it becomes clear that whereas only 5% of semi- and unskilled manual churchgoers live in such a mixed environment, a quarter of them would welcome the opportunity of moving to such a residential context (see Figure 44).

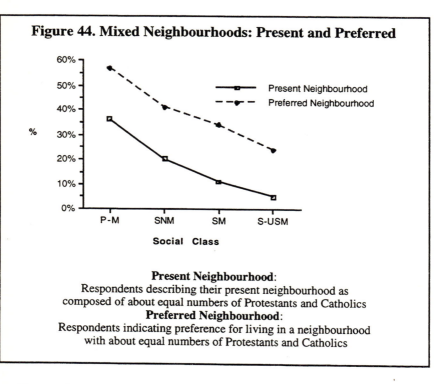

Figure 44. Mixed Neighbourhoods: Present and Preferred

Present Neighbourhood:
Respondents describing their present neighbourhood as composed of about equal numbers of Protestants and Catholics
Preferred Neighbourhood:
Respondents indicating preference for living in a neighbourhood with about equal numbers of Protestants and Catholics

Perceptions of neighbourhood change also vary considerably among the different social class groupings. No doubt this springs in large measure from the character of the neighbourhoods in which respondents find themselves. Those from professional-managerial backgrounds perceive their neighbourhoods to be decidedly more mixed than do those from semi- and unskilled manual households. Alongside this, we discover that 49% of those from professional or managerial backgrounds believe that their neighbourhoods have become considerably more Catholic over the previous five years, compared with 10% for those from semi- and unskilled manual households. It appears that people from working class areas perceive their neighbourhoods to be more stable in terms of religious residential composition than middle class areas, and correspondingly to have experienced less Catholic in-migration (see Figure 45).

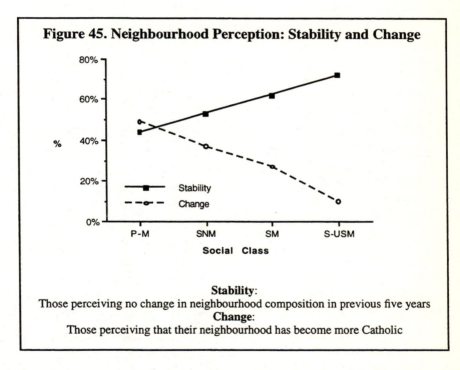

Figure 45. Neighbourhood Perception: Stability and Change

Stability:
Those perceiving no change in neighbourhood composition in previous five years
Change:
Those perceiving that their neighbourhood has become more Catholic

Beyond the residential sphere, attitudes to cross-community matters also surface in a range of other ways—in the educational arena, on the question of mixed marriage, and in the realm of equality of opportunity. So far as education is concerned, the pattern of attitude by social class to aspects of integrated schooling broadly follows the contours of our findings on residential preference. In brief, professional-managerial church attenders are considerably more supportive of sending their children to a school with more or less equal numbers of Protestant and

Catholic pupils (48%) than semi- and unskilled manual churchgoers (28%). Indeed the latter group is decidedly more in favour of educating children in an all-Protestant school (49%) than the former (13%). Beyond the matter of numbers, however, it is clear that throughout the class spectrum, a majority of our respondents prefer to send their children to a school where exclusively Protestant religious values are promulgated. Those supportive of an educational environment with a shared Protestant-Catholic ethos declines from 42% among the professional-managerial to 24% for the semi- and unskilled manual. All this, moreover, is despite the widespread support across all four occupational groups for participating in the less threatening realm of cross-community school projects (P-M 95%; SNM 95%; SM 90%; S-USM 80%).

Not surprisingly, mixed Protestant-Catholic marriage is very substantially opposed by respondents irrespective of social class. Having said that, however, some differences by class are clearly detectable. Whereas 22% of those from professional-managerial backgrounds say that they would be happy to marry a Northern Irish Catholic, the figure drops to 7% for the semi- and unskilled manual. What is interesting is that these figures are remarkably similar to those for attitudes to inter-racial marriage—in this case for Blacks and Chinese. Finally, on the question of fairness within Northern Irish society, we find that, irrespective of social class, Protestant churchgoers overwhelmingly (95%-98% across the class spectrum) express the opinion that 'Catholics generally get a fair deal.' By contrast, the belief that Protestants enjoy fair treatment is not so widely shared by our respondents (from 82% among the professional-managerial class to 67% among the semi- and unskilled manual). Clearly those who are more likely to be socially disadvantaged are less likely to feel that they are being fairly treated in Northern Ireland today.

In brief, it is clear that social class matters a good deal in the production and reproduction of a variety of cross-community attitudes. Because working class membership correlates in some measure with position of the theological spectrum, in all likelihood religious and class values are reciprocally reinforcing.

Politics and Identity

Although there is a considerable variation in attitudes to aspects of cross-community interaction across the class spectrum, when it comes to such matters as national identity and the constitutional future of Northern Ireland the differences are very much more muted. Thus social class seemed to be unimportant in the answers respondents gave to the question of how they would describe themselves. Around 4 out of 10 said they thought of themselves as 'British', while the labels 'Ulsterman/woman' and 'Ulster British' each attracted around 20% of the answers across the class range. The only term that did seem to produce a class-related variation was 'Northern Irish' which was rather more strongly favoured by professional-managerial respondents (19%) than by those from semi- and unskilled manual backgrounds (4%). Having said this, there does seem to be something of a more strongly pro-Ulster sentiment among members of the working class. For example, although the vast majority of respondents preferred the term 'Northern Ireland' to describe their country, 'Ulster' was considerably more favoured by semi- and unskilled manual churchgoers (21%) than by those in the professional-managerial class (7%).

The lack of social class differentiation on the above matters is also evident in Protestant churchgoers' sentiments regarding the long term political future of Northern Ireland. Simply, the overwhelming majority remained convinced that Northern Ireland should remain part of the United Kingdom. Opposition to a united Ireland is thus almost universal. Nevertheless when asked what best explained why Protestants adopt such a viewpoint, there was an interesting divergence of opinion, albeit not significantly distinguished by social class. Fear of the role that the Catholic church would play in a future all-Ireland was the most common answer (36% to 40% across the class divide), with concerns about 'losing their British identity' closely following (28% to 32%). What is remarkable, however, given these persuasions, is that the vast majority (more than three quarters) of churchgoing Protestants—again irrespective of social class—believe that at some point in the future there will be a majority of Catholics in the Northern Ireland population; indeed a significant minority (ranging between 47% and 30% along the class axis) thinks that this situation will have materialised within the next thirty years. It is important to observe in this context, however, that compared with our earlier survey for 1983, the proportion of those expecting a transition to a Catholic majority within thirty years has markedly declined from two thirds to rather less than a half.

Because attitudes to the issues we have just been discussing do not seem to be directly correlated with social class affiliation, this certainly does not mean that class identity is irrelevant in the political arena in Northern Ireland. This is plainly brought out when we consider our findings on party political preference (see Figure 46). What is initially

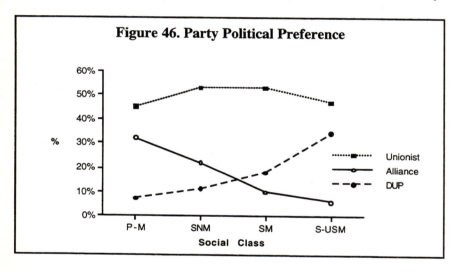

clear, of course, is the broad band of support for the Unionist party across the classes. Beyond this, however, there is a clear indication that class does affect political persuasion with the more middle class elements tending towards the Alliance Party and the working classes favouring the DUP. [14]

---

14. It should be recorded that around 10% of respondents found no political party to their liking.

The staunchly unionist sentiments among the working class that these patterns display draws, for churchgoers, considerable sustenance from their religious identity. One measure of this association centres on the extent to which churchgoers feel that their religious values are intimately bound up with Northern Ireland's constitutional position. To get at this, we asked churchgoers to respond to the statement: 'The Gospel can only flourish in Northern Ireland if it remains separate from the Republic of Ireland.' Across the class range the majority of respondents disagreed with the proposition. But what is noticeable is that a much larger proportion of working class churchgoers agreed with it than was the case with the middle class (from 40% to 12% across the class strata). Clearly it is among the working class that religious and territorial ideology are most tightly interwoven. That this is a *class-related* phenomenon (rather than being determined by allegiance to any one party) is revealed in the fact that those working class respondents agreeing with the proposition were as likely to support the Unionist party as the DUP. No doubt it is for this reason too that while the majority of respondents felt that the Northern Ireland troubles are fundamentally about politics rather than religion, again the larger proportion of those indicating that they felt the problem was about religion came from the working class.

With the more vigorous expressions of support for unionism emanating from those churchgoers among the working class, it is understandable that it is from these same social groupings that the strongest approval for the Orange Order is to be found. While 82% of semi- and unskilled manual churchgoers indicate their approval for the institution, the number falls to 46% for professional/managerial—indeed if we isolate the professional segment of this latter grouping we find that support here further declines to 38%. Perhaps this support for the Orange Order, a unifying Protestant institution, is connected with the fact that working class respondents are much more likely than their middle class counterparts to think that the Catholic community is strongly united even though it is true that all the social groups are more inclined to perceive that the Catholic community enjoys greater solidarity than their own (see Figure 47).

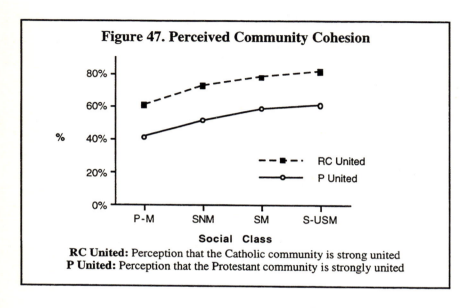

Figure 47. Perceived Community Cohesion

RC United: Perception that the Catholic community is strong united
P United: Perception that the Protestant community is strongly united

In contrast to political life in many other situations in the Western world, class affiliation—at least on the surface—does not seem to make much difference to the attitudes taken up to large scale political questions, questions which are intimately connected with matters of identity. However, when we probe a little further, it becomes clear that there are indeed a diverse range of identities expressed by the different social classes. This suggests that the uniform constitutional stance that Protestant churchgoers of all classes in Belfast project may spring from a diverging set of cultural, religious, and social aspirations. A monolithic outcome must not be taken to imply an underlying cultural singularity. That there is indeed a plurality is attested to by the diversity of class-based religious experience which we have uncovered (for there are important ties linking class structure and denominational/theological pattern), and by the differing class-distinguished stances disclosed in attitudes towards ecumenical matters and cross-community relations more generally. What is here manifest in terms of social class, perhaps, is a range of Ulster unionisms stretching from a more exclusivist stance which retains aspirations toward politico-religious 'purity' to a more inclusivist outlook hoping to incorporate a stronger cross-communitarianism within a broader unionist *méntalité*. It is therefore appropriate now to turn, finally, to the role of political affinity within churchgoing Protestantism.

Political Affinity

The general pattern of party political preference among our respondents and the broad demographic characteristics thereof have been reviewed, as has the relationship between party political preference and denomination affiliation. Besides these there are significant connections between political orientation and such social dimensions as educational attainment and class. As for the former, our findings reveal that for both the Unionist and Democratic Unionist parties support among churchgoers is predominantly drawn from those who completed their education at the primary or secondary level. This is especially true for the DUP (71% compared with 53% for Unionists). Correspondingly, the Alliance party draws much greater support from those with a university education, 41% compared with 16% and 7% for the Unionist and Democratic Unionist parties respectively. This pattern is further reflected in general terms in the social class composition of party support. Accordingly, the Alliance Party displays a strongly middle class character with 63% being derived from a professional-managerial background, compared with 40% for Unionists, and 22% for DUP. At the opposite end of the class scale, the DUP derives its support proportionately more from semi- and unskilled manual churchgoers (29%) than is the case with Unionists (11%) or Alliance (4%).

Politics and Religion
Party political affinity, it is clear from our findings, directly bears on the practices of religious life. For example, DUP supporters are much more likely than their Alliance counterparts to attend church twice on a Sunday (69% compared with 39%). This pattern of religiosity predictably finds expression in a range of related religious practices. Twice

daily prayer and daily Bible reading, for instance, equally follow the contours of party preference. In these cases the most ardent practitioners are drawn from the DUP, followed by Unionist and then Alliance. No doubt these findings reflect the strongly conversionist ethic that pervades the worldview of churchgoers with a DUP inclination; 87% of them claim to have undergone a personal conversion experience, while 90% insist that conversion is crucial to genuine Christianity. By contrast the corresponding figures for Alliance advocates are 54% and 47% respectively with, as before, the Unionist segment occupying a position between these extremes (68% and 67%). On matters of biblical interpretation, a similar pattern surfaces. DUP turn out to be the most inerrantist in their views (86%) and also the most likely to insist on a literal reading of biblical texts (78%). In both cases figures for those with Alliance sympathies are dramatically lower—30% and 21%. By now a composite image of the religious convictions of the different political parties is clearly emerging and is encapsulated in Figure 48.

Democratic Unionist churchgoers are evidently the most religiously conservative in belief and observant in practice of the three parties; those with Alliance affinities clearly adopt rather a more liberal viewpoint on certain beliefs and are less assiduous in practice; in all this the Unionists seem to occupy the middle ground. In general terms there is doubtless something correct about these stereotypes. But stereotypes they assuredly are, for it must be remembered that for every indicator we have examined there are a considerable number of respondents who do not neatly fit the typology.

The conservative religious tendencies that these findings portray also emerge in attitudes to one of the more recent controversial aspects of modern religious life, namely, the role of women in churches. In general terms, those groups displaying higher levels of religious observance are also those more closely associated with social traditionalism.

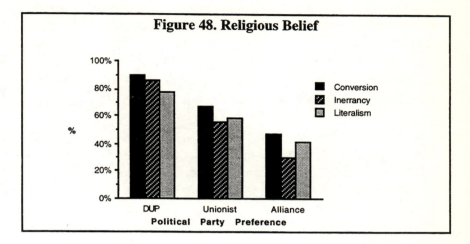

Figure 48. Religious Belief

Attitudes to a variety of roles that women might perform within churches—women clergy, women elders, and women preaching—thus vary considerably by political preference (see Figure 49).

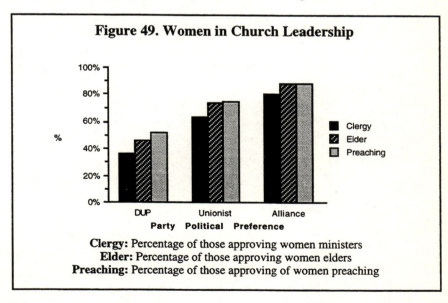

Figure 49. Women in Church Leadership

Clergy: Percentage of those approving women ministers
Elder: Percentage of those approving women elders
Preaching: Percentage of those approving of women preaching

Views about the use of inclusive language in Bible reading similarly follow this pattern of response. The use of the word 'humankind' as opposed to 'man' finds favour with only a minority of respondents across the political spectrum; nevertheless where approval is expressed, it is much more likely to emanate from those with Alliance Party inclinations (41%) than from either Unionist (27%) or DUP (11%).

Politics and Social Change

The above comments on changing attitudes to the role of women within the church serves to introduce some of the broader issues of social change to which society has been exposed in recent years. Undoubtedly one of the most significant of these changes has centred on the shifting patterns of female employment. Given the different political ideologies that our respondents have been expressing thus far, it is noteworthy that attitudes to women in the workplace do *not* seem to be significantly differentiated by political party preference, though—as we pointed out in our 'General Overview'—there have been considerable attitudinal shifts towards greater acceptance in the past decade. Thus we find that the vast majority of respondents regardless of party political affinity are supportive of women without children going out to work. Less approval is expressed for women with school-age children entering employment though some three quarters are nonetheless supportive. In the case of women with children under school age the attitudes of Protestant churchgoers are dramatically different. Only a minority from all the political stances are approving of women working in such circumstances, though it is significant that the strongest expression of support is derived from those who favour the Alliance Party (48% compared with around a third for the other two parties).

By contrast, party political orientation makes a very considerable difference to attitudes expressed concerning disciplinary aspects of social regulation. Alliance party supporters are much less enthusiastic about the reintroduction of corporal punishment in schools and much less supportive of capital punishment. On what is perceived as greater leniency in court sentencing, there is a substantial concern across the party range, though here too it is somewhat less marked among Alliance sympathisers (see Figure 50).

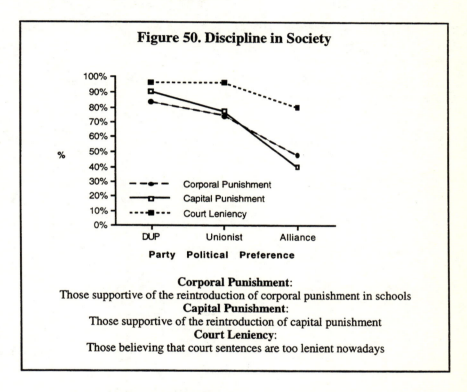

Figure 50. Discipline in Society

Corporal Punishment:
Those supportive of the reintroduction of corporal punishment in schools
Capital Punishment:
Those supportive of the reintroduction of capital punishment
Court Leniency:
Those believing that court sentences are too lenient nowadays

A somewhat similar expression of what might be called social conservatism also surfaces in the attitudes adopted by the different political groupings to an issue of traditional concern in Northern Ireland, namely, Sunday observance. Here the difference by political preference is striking. Attendance at a Sunday sports event, while opposed by a majority of respondents from all political persuasions, does find considerably stronger support among those with Alliance sympathies (37%) compared with Unionists (16%) and Democratic Unionists (8%). Again resistance to watching television on Sunday remains most solid for DUP churchgoers with only 51% doing so, compared with 81% of Unionists and 93% Alliance.

Not surprisingly these self-same patterns are equally expressed in attitudes towards a variety of other matters to do with public and private morality. Figure 51 displays our findings for stances adopted by those of different political persuasions on premarital sex, cohabitation before marriage, abortion, homosexuality, and divorce. In every case the DUP displays a higher level of moral strictness than the other two parties, with Alliance consistently showing a greater proportion of respondents adopting a less rigorous moral stance.

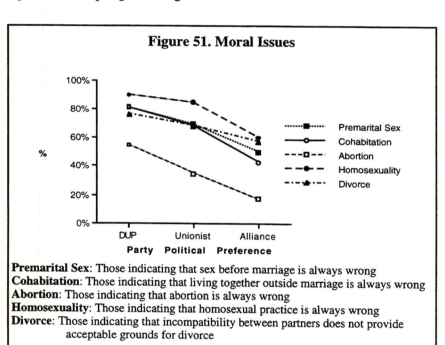

Premarital Sex: Those indicating that sex before marriage is always wrong
Cohabitation: Those indicating that living together outside marriage is always wrong
Abortion: Those indicating that abortion is always wrong
Homosexuality: Those indicating that homosexual practice is always wrong
Divorce: Those indicating that incompatibility between partners does not provide acceptable grounds for divorce

Taken overall, there is evidence to support the view that political affinity is correlated with a variety of attitudes to recent social change. By and large the DUP maintain the most socially conservative stance on issues to do with the role of women, sexual mores, and public order, and thereby display a rather more punitive mindset compared with Alliance supporters who are consistently more liberal—and consequently more lenient—in social ideology. In most cases the Unionists occupy a more middle-of-the-road position.

Political Ideology and Cross-Community Interaction
Given that our study centres on Belfast churchgoers, it is appropriate to begin our analysis of the impact of political orientation on cross-community concerns by focusing initially on the more purely 'religious' components of the question. Thus when we examine the *experience* of ecumenical services of worship by the different political groupings we find a huge difference. While only 14% of DUP have ever participated in such a church service, the figure dramatically rises to 76% for Alliance, with the Unionists occupying a middle position—39%. No doubt this is related, at least in part, to the question of opportunity to participate in such ventures, and we will make some comments presently on the neighbourhood characteristics of these different political groups. Nonetheless, there are clear indications that attitude is more important that availability on this issue. For example, when asked about their willingness to engage in joint services of worship with Roman Catholics, a mere 9% of DUP responded in the affirmative compared with 30% of Unionists and 76% of Alliance.

In this connection it is interesting to compare these findings with attitudes towards joint services with Free Presbyterians. Support for joining in worship with Free Presbyterians stands at 40% for Alliance and 49% for Unionists. Predictably 78% of DUP welcomed such opportunities; though it should be noted that this means that 22% of Democratic Unionists are *not* enthusiastic about participating in joint worship services with the Free Presbyterian Church.[15] Clearly Free Presbyterianism and Democratic Unionism do not neatly map on to each other.

Given the relative enthusiasm for inter-church relations expressed by Alliance supporters, it is understandable that, of all the parties, they

---

15. Six sevenths of this 22% are from denominations other than the Free Presbyterian Church.

should be most in favour of the churches becoming much more active in fostering community relations (79%). By contrast the Unionists and Democratic Unionists are less keen that churches should pursue such objectives with 55% and 46% respectively urging much greater cross-community activity. Of course this does mean that around a half of these two latter groups *are* supportive of such ventures, and this is in line with the expressed willingness of both Unionists (40%) and Democratic Unionists (49%) to see greater social cooperation between the Protestant and Catholic churches. That these groupings are less willing than the Alliance to pursue both religious and social interaction is now predictable. Yet we should record that while religious and social cooperation finds support from 46% of Unionists, the figure falls to 19% of DUP, largely because 28% of them do not want any links with the Catholic Church whatsoever.[16]

The findings we have just reported clearly reveal that there are highly significant and complex relations between political outlook and religious faith. It is frequently thought, however, that the interweaving of political ideology and religious conviction is a particularly dominant motif in the Democratic Unionist mindset. Our findings, at least to some extent, query this conventional portrayal. For when asked how they would react to greater social and political comment on Northern Ireland's problems in sermons, the Alliance contingent was, by far, the most supportive. Eighty-seven per cent of them favoured sermons dealing with social and economic issues compared with 62% of Unionists and 54% of DUP, with a similar pattern, at a slightly lower level, being revealed for sermons dealing with political matters. All this suggests a greater concern to integrate what might be called the 'spiritual' and the 'secular' among Alliance than among the other two groupings. In all likelihood, of course, the moral and spiritual values that the different political groups espouse in their desire to keep faith and politics in tandem are very different; but that these connections

---

16. The comparable figure for Unionists not wanting greater cooperation on anything is 8% and for Alliance only 1%.

should exist is widely shared by churchgoers across the political spectrum.

The pattern of these attitudes towards the more ecclesiastical aspects of cross-community interaction finds further confirmation in the active participation of churchgoers in cross-community organisations. The most extensive involvement (36%) was registered by those with Alliance sympathies, with the proportion declining to 15% for Unionists and 8% for DUP. At least in part, this pattern (and indeed the earlier structure of cross-community attitudes we have discerned) may reflect the neighbourhood context within which respondents reside. A distinctive residential geography of churchgoers differentiated by political persuasion is evident (see Figure 52).

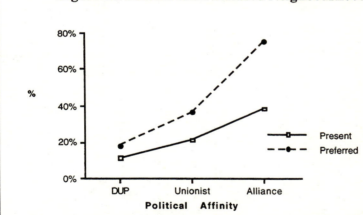

Figure 52. Present and Preferred Neighbourhood

Present: Those describing their present neighbourhood as having equal numbers of Protestants and Catholics
Preferred: Those indicating a preference for living in a neighbourhood with equal numbers of Protestants and Catholics

What emerges is that those residing in a residential environment with an equal mix of Protestants and Catholics are rather more likely to be of Alliance persuasion; conversely the all-Protestant neighbourhood is decidedly more a DUP phenomenon. It seems plausible, therefore, to suggest that these differing host environments may play a not insignificant role in the reproduction of social attitudes towards members of the other community. What is more, there is clear evidence to suggest that not only is this residential pattern correlated with political outlook, but also that the desire for residential mixing is substantially more marked among those with Alliance allegiances.

Given the fact that neighbourhoods are strongly class distinguished, it is interesting to consider the issue of the links between religious belief and social class across the different political parties. When asked whether respondents had 'more in common with' a Catholic of their own class or a Protestant of a different class, the responses were strongly marked by political affiliation. The two unionist parties were much more likely than the Alliance to identify with religious allegiance rather than class membership; for the Alliance it was the opposite, namely, they were much more inclined to have a sense of class solidarity irrespective of religious persuasion (see Figure 53).

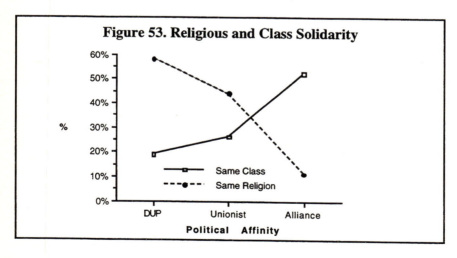

In the wider domain of cross-community relations significant differences are also discernible in attitudes towards mixed Protestant-Catholic education and mixed marriage (see Figure 54).

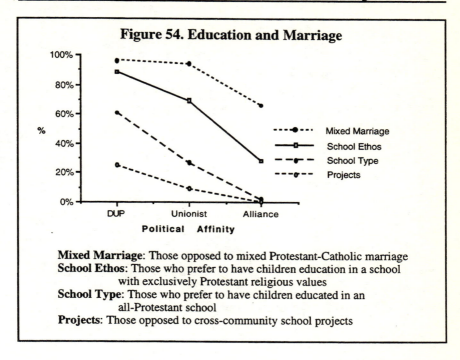

Figure 54. Education and Marriage

Mixed Marriage: Those opposed to mixed Protestant-Catholic marriage
School Ethos: Those who prefer to have children education in a school with exclusively Protestant religious values
School Type: Those who prefer to have children educated in an all-Protestant school
Projects: Those opposed to cross-community school projects

Here the same solidarities that we have just observed among those of different political persuasions surface again in these arenas. When we examine the type of school to which respondents would prefer to send their children in terms of its population balance and its religious ethos, and when we examine attitudes towards the pursuance of cross-community school projects, a predictable gradient from DUP through Unionist to Alliance clearly expresses itself. Attitudes to mixed Protestant-Catholic marriage follow a similar pattern albeit at a much higher level of opposition across the political range. Figure 54 presents the responses of churchgoers differentiated by political affinity to this diverse range of social mixing in the educational and marital spheres.

Finally, the question of equity in Northern Irish society stimulated a diverse set of responses from churchgoers according to their political outlook. Overall there is a widespread feeling that Catholics in Northern Ireland get a fair deal these days (98% of Unionists, 98% of DUP, and 91% of Alliance). However, a sense of injustice towards

Protestants was clearly registered by the DUP only 49% of whom agreed that Protestants are fairly treated in contemporary Northern Ireland. Among Unionists this figure rose to 75%, and to 91% for Alliance. Evidently feelings of discrimination are more strongly felt by DUP churchgoers than by those of the other two political groups. Insofar as there is something called Protestant 'alienation', it seems most likely to be felt by those of DUP persuasion.

Party political affiliation, plainly, crystallises a diverse range of attitudes towards cross-community matters. Those churchgoers with a firm commitment to furthering interaction between Protestants and Catholics in a variety of spheres, would appear to find the Alliance Party the most congenial to their political tastes. By contrast, expressions of religious and social separatism are more forthcoming from those with DUP sympathies. Most churchgoers, of course, lie somewhere between these polarities, and this is expressed in the substantial majority support for the Unionist party. Characterising our findings in this way, of course, has its dangers and the inclination towards stereotyping must be resisted. On every cross-community issue we have scrutinised there are sometimes considerable minorities who do not follow the general pattern.

Political Persuasion and National Identity
In contrast to the issues we have just been scrutinising, the impact of political conviction on matters to do with identity turns out to be rather more muted. To be sure there are expressions of difference, not least on attitudes towards the Orange Order—on which we will presently comment; but overall these are rather less dramatic than the disparities we have been charting thus far.

Turning first to the nomenclature of national identity that respondents specify to designate themselves, we find that there is only a marginal difference among the political groupings in the use of 'British' as the preferred label. Beyond that, it is noticeable that the Unionists (40%) and Democratic Unionists (56%) are rather more inclined to opt for a description that incorporates an Ulster dimension—either Ulsterman/woman, or Ulster British.[17] By contrast those with Alliance affinities are rather more prone to use the term 'Northern Irish' in their response (27% compared with 9% and 4% for the other two parties). The fact that a majority of respondents irrespective of political party preference do not choose to describe themselves solely as 'British' seems not unrelated to the perception that is shared across the political spectrum that people in Britain either do not understand the Northern Ireland situation at all, or have very little comprehension why 'many Ulster Protestants want to maintain the union.' In all cases the percentages are around 90.

When it comes to assessing why it is that Protestants object to a United Ireland, fear of the role of the Catholic church in a future all-Ireland is the most commonly specified answer among both Unionists and Democratic Unionists, and is particularly emphasised among the latter. Among Alliance churchgoers, their diagnosis is equally split between fear of the Catholic Church and the loss of a British identity.

On other matters connected with nationhood in Northern Ireland there are, overall, only marginal differences between the various political allegiances. For example, a widespread feeling exists (over three quarters of each grouping) that at a time in the future more than half the population of Northern Ireland will be Catholic, and a shared sense amongst about a half of respondents that this changeover is likely to come about within a generation. Again, there is a unifying belief that the future of Northern Ireland should be to remain part of the United Kingdom, though this is a little less strongly felt by those of Alliance outlook.

And yet for all these shared expressions of identity and aspiration, variations may still strongly surface. Consider the diverse range of attitudes towards the Orange Order. Approval of this organisation is widespread among DUP supporters (standing at 90%) and Unionists (75%); by contrast only 21% of Alliance sympathisers find it congenial.

---

17. The comparable Alliance figure is 26%.

Paradoxically, given the fact that the Orange Order is frequently seen as a unifying institution within an otherwise diverse Protestant community, it is of significance that the group most likely to sense fragmentation among Protestants is the Alliance—the very group least approving of the Orange Order. Whereas only 33% of them believe that 'the Protestant community is strongly united', 55% of Unionists and 60% of Democratic Unionists are convinced of the truth of this assertion.

The Northern Ireland polity is frequently depicted as a latter-day theocracy. The findings we have here disclosed certainly do reveal that there are intimate connections between political affinity and religious conviction. These, however, are subtle and diverse, and express themselves rather differently on different issues across the various political ideologies. And yet when it comes to the straight question of the identification of religious faith with geographical territory a majority of all respondents deny the connection. When asked to react to the statement that 'the Gospel can only flourish in Northern Ireland if it remains separate from the Republic of Ireland', there was only agreement from a minority in each of the political sectors. The strongest body of support for the statement emerges from those of a DUP disposition (42%), with only a handful of Alliance sympathisers (7%) adopting such a stance. For some, in conclusion, geographical space and religious identity remain firmly intertwined; for them there is an intimate connection between territory and theology such that the preservation of the theology requires the maintenance of the geography. For others territory and theology can not, and should not, follow the same contours; to them grace and space simply do not belong together.

Party political orientation is of considerable significance in accounting for the attitudinal variation displayed amongst Protestant churchgoers in Belfast. For a start, each of the political parties displays a distinctive religious topography in terms of denominational and theological profile. In addition, significant variation by party is conspicuous on issues to do with cross-community relations, women's concerns, private morality, and the regulation of the public sphere. Of course these attitudinal patterns are not exclusively the product of political allegiance. They are also the outcome of a complex web of additional factors such as social class and religious conviction. Yet what does become clear is that, for all this variety, on the question of the constitutional future of Northern Ireland Protestant churchgoers very largely speak with one voice. All this contributes towards a condition to which we have already adverted, namely, that a unified political aspiration may spring from a diverse set of religious and social aspirations. Indeed it may well be the case that Protestant churchgoers, taken overall, believe that it is only within one particular constitutional polity—the United Kingdom—that they can find an acceptable space, both metaphorical and material, within which their diversity can find expression.

Conclusion: A Majority of Minorities

While Protestants in Belfast, as in Northern Ireland more generally, find themselves forming a majority of the population, religiously at least they are fragmented into a series of denominational groupings, each—therefore—a 'minority within a majority'. As our findings have shown, moreover, denominational variation is certainly not the only way in which churchgoing Protestantism may be disaggregated. Position on a theological spectrum from conservative to liberal, social class membership, demographic structure, congregational affiliation, stances on public morality, and attitudes towards cross-community relations are just some of the other ways in which the Protestant churchgoing population is divided. The identity of Protestant churchgoers, we therefore contend, is composed of a multi-layering of constituent elements which come together in different ways to produce widely varying renditions of 'the Protestant churchgoer'.

To acknowledge this fragmentation, however, is not to deny the reality of a Protestant culture; rather it is to point to its essentially contested character. Perhaps this is most clearly apparent in questions to do with the constitutional future of Northern Ireland. On this issue churchgoing Protestants, it is clear, overwhelmingly speak with one voice. Yet this constitutional coalescence may well arise from a plurality of motivations. Indeed it seems to be the case that there is a Protestant sense that it is only within one specific set of constitutional arrangements that their diversity can find expression. If this is so, a monolithic political objective turns out to be nothing less than the manifestation of a contested, and therefore vital, tradition. For vital traditions, in contrast to moribund cultures, as Alasdair MacIntyre (1985, p. 222) has argued, 'embody continuities of conflict.'

IV

'Them and Us': Sameness And Difference

General Introduction

Having scrutinised the internal continuities and discontinuities within each of the Catholic and Protestant churchgoing populations, we now turn to a comparison across the same two populations. Our aim is to provide an overall sense of the characteristics of churchgoers, both Protestant and Catholic, so often portrayed as two discrete traditions. We will tease out the ways in which their respective religious and social experiences converge or diverge, and seek to show how age, theological profession, social class type, political affiliation and so on condition attitudes to a variety of issues. The possibilities for analysis here are almost infinite. And so we have had to be selective in the choice of items we have chosen to examine. The findings we present are thus deliberately intended to be illustrative rather than exhaustive, suggestive rather than comprehensive.

People Profile

So far as matters of gender and age are concerned, there is an altogether remarkable similarity between Catholic and Protestant churchgoers. For Catholics and Protestants, churchgoing is a predominately female activity, with both populations returning 59% female and 41% male. Since, as we will now see, people in the upper age brackets are more likely to be church attenders, one might expect, therefore, that this gender bias is reflective of the age structure of churchgoing populations. This, however, is not the case; in virtually every age cohort females predominate in similar proportions to the overall gender ratio.

While the age structures of both churchgoing communities are, as we have indicated, remarkably similar, there are indications that Protestant churchgoers, on average, belong to a somewhat older age group (see Figure 55). This is evident in the proportion of them in the over 65 age category—40% compared with 33% for Catholics.

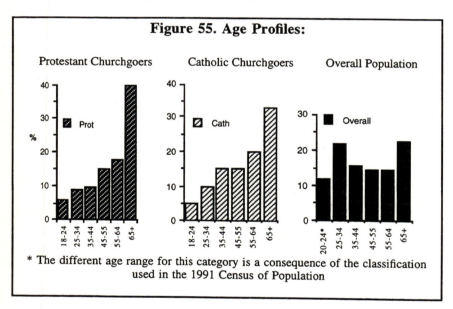

Figure 55. Age Profiles:

* The different age range for this category is a consequence of the classification used in the 1991 Census of Population

What comes through clearly from our overall findings, however, is that churchgoing across the religious divide is predominantly an older-age phenomenon. When we compare the age profile of Protestant and Catholic churchgoers with that of the population as a whole in the Belfast District Council Area what is immediately striking is the similarity of the two churchgoing structures to each other, and the fundamental contrast between them and the overall population age distribution.

As with age profile, Catholic and Protestant churchgoers share a broadly similar social class structure. Where there are differences these are to be found at the extremities of the social class spectrum. While 15% of Protestant churchgoers may be classified as professional, the figure falls to 7% among Catholics; for those in the managerial category the respective figures are, for Protestants, 25% and, for Catholics, 22%. Again, whereas only 4% of Protestants are unskilled, the corresponding Catholic figure is 8%.

These are not major differences, however, and what is striking is the overall similarity compared with the social class structure of Belfast as a whole. When we group together the professional and managerial occupational categories we find that, for Belfast overall, the figure is 6%; this compares with around 40% of Protestant churchgoers and around 30% of Catholic churchgoers. It is possible, of course, that our respondents were disproportionately drawn from the middle class because they may have been more accustomed to dealing with documentation and were thus more likely to complete and return the questionnaire. This is undoubtedly a value judgement and may be incorrect. Nevertheless, even if this is so, we are convinced that churchgoing, whether Protestant or Catholic, is, disproportionately, a middle class activity.

Parallels between Protestant and Catholic churchgoers are also evident in their perceptions of social mobility as reflected in the comparison between perceived current social class and perceived social class of the home background. In general, people have a sense that there has been an inter-generational drift away from manual occupations to white collar jobs. Overall, to put it another way, there is a widespread perception among churchgoers that they have experienced some upward social mobility. What we also find is that this experience is more or less equally shared by both Catholic and Protestant churchgoers.

The pattern of unemployment displayed among our respondents is also similar. For Belfast churchgoing Protestants, long-term and short-term unemployment stands at 3%, among Catholics it is just under 6%. This compares with over 11% unemployment for the

Belfast District Council area overall (see Figure 56). Clearly current churchgoers are, proportionately, somewhat less likely to experience unemployment than the population as a whole. This situation, of course, is likely to be affected by the substantially larger proportion

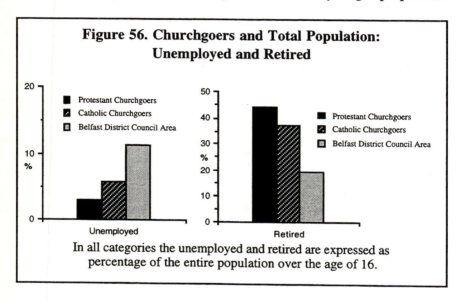

Figure 56. Churchgoers and Total Population: Unemployed and Retired

In all categories the unemployed and retired are expressed as percentage of the entire population over the age of 16.

of churchgoers, both Catholic and Protestant, who are retired. From a demographic point of view, then, Belfast's churchgoing Protestants and Catholics have much in common. We must now consider whether this similarity translates into behaviour and attitudes.

Faith And Practice

In matters of faith and practice we find both continuities and discontinuities between our Catholic and Protestant respondents. Perhaps the most striking finding uniting Belfast Protestant and Catholic churchgoers is the remarkably high level of commitment to the classical doctrines of the church. Similarly, there is no difference between the two churchgoing traditions on the matter of private prayer with 78% of both groups engaging in daily prayer. Whereas on these aspects of faith and practice there is substantial agreement, a marked divergence emerges over the centrality of religious conversion and the frequency of Bible reading. While 68% of Protestants report a 'turning point' in their lives when they committed themselves to Christ, this is true for only 34% of Catholics. However the question was interpreted, we can at least conclude that Protestants share a much more pronounced conversionist culture than churchgoing Catholics. In addition, Protestant churchgoers are much more Bible-oriented than their Catholic counterparts, with nearly half reading it once a day and 14% doing so several times a week. By contrast, less than one in ten Catholics read scripture on a daily basis, and 37% never read it at all in private.[1] It is clear that the Reformation heritage of *Sola Scriptura* continues to find expression in the every-day religious lives of Belfast Protestant churchgoers.

If it might indeed be said, then, that Protestant churchgoers are people of 'the book', it could be claimed that Catholic churchgoers are people of a community of faith. Some confirmation of this sense of community might be found in the contrast between the two groups' means of getting to their places of worship. The fact that 60% of Catholics, compared with only 20% of Protestants, walk to church is itself evidence of a much more robust experience of parish life among the former. Protestant churchgoing is plainly more markedly characterised by 'commuting' than its Catholic counterpart. While 73% of Protestants come to church by car, for Catholics the figure is only 36%, the difference being explained less by social class than by proximity of Catholics to their places of worship. Clearly the opportunities for neighbourhood interaction are much greater where walking to and from church is the dominant mode of travel, and this undoubtedly acts to reinforce any sense of parish identity and community. Besides, our findings indicate that

---

1. An added dimension to this may be divergent attitudes to the nature of the Bible, with 52% of Protestant churchgoers reporting that 'Every passage in the Bible should be taken literally,' compared with 30% of Catholics.

Protestants are decidedly more willing to pass many places of worship, even those of their own denomination, to attend a church which is to their liking. Of course the sheer availability of Protestant inter- and intra-denominational variety itself contributes to these patterns. What further reinforces this sense of Protestant mobility is the fact that Protestants churchgoers are, predictably, far more likely than Catholics to have crossed denominational divides. Thus only 70% of Protestants report that they have always been connected with their current denomination, compared with 99% of Catholics.

Women's Issues

On one issue of considerable contemporary debate there is a marked divergence of opinion between Catholic and Protestant churchgoers (see Figure 57). While some two thirds of Protestants express

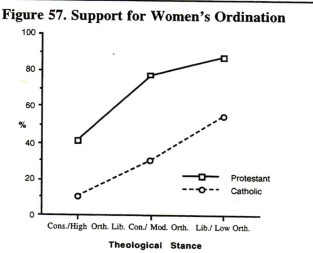

Figure 57. Support for Women's Ordination

The theological categories are, for Protestants: **conservative, liberal-conservative, liberal**; for Catholics: **high orthodoxy, moderate orthodoxy, low orthodoxy**

approval for the ordination of women, the figure drops to only one quarter of churchgoing Catholics. These findings, it turns out, are closely connected with respondents' theological convictions. Whereas a mere 10% of highly orthodox Catholics favour women's ordination, the figure rises to 55% for those of low orthodoxy. Correspondingly, 87% of Protestant liberals support women clergy compared with 41% of conservatives.

This response, moreover, is highly age dependent. In a nutshell, older Catholics (those over the age of 65) are vigorously opposed to women's ordination (only 10% give their approval); older Protestants, by contrast, are strongly in favour (71%). At the other end of the age spectrum there is little divergence between the communities with 42% of Catholics and 49% of Protestants under the age of 35 giving their support to women clergy. This of course means that the relative support within each group is coming from the opposite ends of the age spectrum: women's ordination is most strongly favoured by older Protestants and younger Catholics.

Given the findings presented above, it seems ironic that efforts to remove gendered language from scripture seem to attract greater support from Catholics. When given the choice between hearing the words 'man' or 'humankind' in scripture reading, 70% of Protestants favoured the former, compared with 42% of Catholics. On the women's question, it seems, Catholics favour linguistic inclusiveness but clerical exclusiveness while with Protestants it is the other way around. What is noteworthy, however, is that whether in attitudes to the ordination of women or to the use of inclusive language it makes little difference for both Protestants and Catholics whether the respondent is male or female.

While questions to do with the role of women *within the church context* elicit considerable difference of opinion between churchgoing Catholics and Protestants, when it comes to more general questions, such as attitudes to women going out to work, what is striking is the remarkable similarity between both populations. Figure 58 reveals the parallel attitudes on women working under a variety of family circumstances.

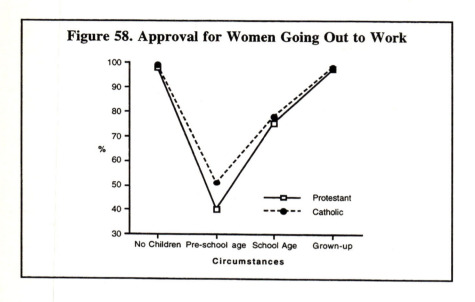

Figure 58. Approval for Women Going Out to Work

The Moral Sphere

In large measure Belfast churchgoers, whether Catholic or Protestant, inhabit a broadly similar moral universe. On a wide range of issues to do with sexual ethics, for example, there is little diversity of opinion. Premarital sexual relations are condemned as always wrong by around two thirds of both communities, and homosexual activities are repudiated by 81% of churchgoing Protestants and 70% of churchgoing Catholics. Correspondingly, both communities seem rather more tolerant of divorce than might initially be expected. Only around 1 in 5 Catholics affirm that divorce is unacceptable in any circumstances, while for Protestants the figure is less than 1 in 10. Moreover, save for one significant difference, there are similar levels of agreement on the circumstances which would justify divorce. Absolute rejection of divorce, as we have said, is uncommon. What *is* noticeable is that Protestants and Catholics have very different attitudes towards adultery as providing acceptable grounds for marital dissolution. Two thirds of churchgoing

Protestants regard adultery as legitimising the case for divorce, compared with only one third of Catholics. To put it another way, Catholics seem less intolerant of adultery than do Protestants.

Predictably there is also very considerable divergence on the abortion question (see Figure 59). When invited to make an initial

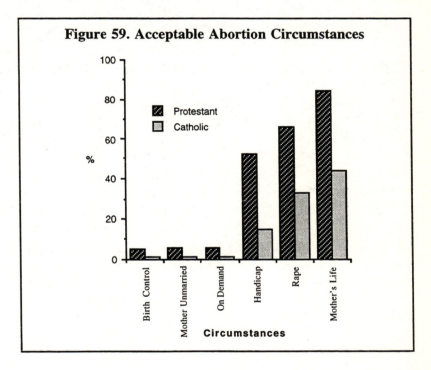

moral judgement on abortion, 36% of churchgoing Protestants register an 'always wrong' response, compared with almost 80% of Catholics. Yet, when confronted with a range of 'real world' circumstances that typically bear on abortion, both Protestants and Catholics exhibit rather less absolutist positions. For example, despite the 80% anti-abortion Catholic response cited above, 44% would find it legally acceptable when 'it is the only way to save the mother's life,' and 33% take the same stance when the 'pregnancy is the result of rape.' Similarly, while 36% of Protestants initially claim that abortion is 'always wrong', when it comes to the saving of the mother's life, 84% find this an acceptable circumstance for the legal availability of abortion. Any divergence in response indicated here may be explained by the suggestion that churchgoers, while keen to express a firm anti-abortion ethic, are, however, prepared to tolerate it in the most extreme circumstance. Despite the clear differences in the ethics of abortion displayed in the figure above, sight should not be lost of the remarkable parallel between Catholics' and Protestants' ranking of the circumstances in which abortion may legitimately occur.

When we probe this issue a little further, moreover, we find a notable coalition of anti-abortion sentiments among those who, in many other respects, are doctrinally antipathetic to each other. Namely, theologically conservative Protestants adopt a position much closer to the Catholic stance on abortion, and, if anything, to the more highly orthodox component of that community.[2]

Because Protestant and Catholic churchgoers espouse many similar—and conservative—moral values does not mean, of course, that there are no appreciable differences in their outlook on certain matters of ethical concern to society. Using a composite measurement drawn from respondents' attitudes to caning in schools, leniency in the courts, and capital punishment it is possible to distinguish those who may be described as socially conservative from their liberal counterparts. Simply, the socially conservative express the following views: corporal punishment should be reintroduced in schools; courts let wrongdoers off too lightly nowadays; and capital punishment should be allowed in certain circumstances. Correspondingly, social liberals reject these propositions. Protestant churchgoers, it turns out, are considerably more disciplinarian than

---

2. 75% of Protestant churchgoers who report that abortion is 'always wrong' are theologically conservative, even though conservatives only comprise 51% of the overall Protestant response. The anti-abortion bias of the highly orthodox on the Catholic side, while present, is much less marked, reflective no doubt of the overall Catholic stance on this moral issue.

their Catholic counterparts with three-quarters of them tending towards the conservative side of the social-moral spectrum compared with only 4 out of 10 Catholics. Indeed, the decided support in Protestant quarters for capital punishment mirrors their general social strictness while the views of Catholics on the matter make one mindful of their pro-life concerns already noted in respect of private morality. The Catholic stance overall may reflect the less rigid and more forgiving tradition of post-Vatican 2 theology, a point raised by Dunlop (1995, p 99) when he notes that 'the Catholic culture of hospitality is gentler and more accommodating with sinners.'

Another public matter of continuing social and, indeed, political concern is the question of Sunday observance (see Figure 60). Despite the general persistence of a strong, often legally buttressed, Sunday observance ethic overall, the contrast between Protestants

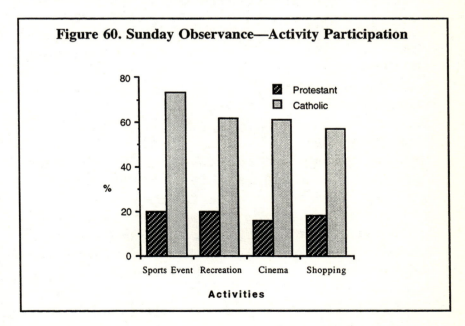

Figure 60. Sunday Observance—Activity Participation

and Catholics is stark. No more than 20% of Protestants are prepared to take part in recreational activities, go to the cinema, attend a sports event or shop despite an environment where these options have become available. Catholic responses suggest that a major culture difference may exist for 60% of the Catholic churchgoing population at least; they are prepared for participation in any of the above activities. The traditional conflict over Sunday closures of children's playgrounds and of leisure centres as well as the more recent campaign against Sunday shopping legislation both highlight the tensions that can ensue when variations in sabbatarian attitudes are pronounced.

Neighbourhood Space

Given the geographical, historical and cultural context of Belfast it is no surprise that religion became, and continues to be, the salient division on which neighbourhood identity depends. The city's neighbourhoods are finely defined, moreover, on the basis of religious composition. Thus, for example, the city has neighbourhoods which are perceived to be entirely Protestant or entirely Catholic, mostly Protestant or mostly Catholic, or to have Protestants and Catholics in more or less equal numbers, and it is these which provide the arena for residential decisions.

Judging from their residential patterns and preferences as described by our churchgoers there is a marked attraction to segregated living. Whether Protestant or Catholic, they are most likely to perceive themselves to be living in areas where their neighbours are all or mostly of the same religion as themselves (70% and 84% respectively). An upbringing in a segregated area for 6 out of 10 Protestants and 7 out of 10 Catholics undoubtedly contributes to such residential outcomes. Indeed, only a quarter of Catholics and a third of Protestants consider that they have grown up in areas where the numbers of Protestants and Catholics were around about equal.

This residential experience, together with the undoubted physical and psychological security offered by segregated living especially during the communal tensions of the last two decades, may partly explain the continuing attractions of religiously defined clustering. Even when given the option of indicating which type of neighbourhood they would actually prefer to live in, more that half of both Protestants and Catholics—57% and 55% respectively—still opt to be entirely or predominantly with their own kind.

The strong attraction for Catholics of religiously exclusive areas both in terms of their free choice and in the description given of their present neighbourhood (6 out of 10 compared to 2 out of 10 Protestants) deserves comment. In addition to the possible contributory factors already considered might be added the Catholic experience over the last twenty five years. Among churchgoers, Catholics are three times more likely to have been intimidated and twice as likely to have had their homes bombed as Protestants (Figure 61).

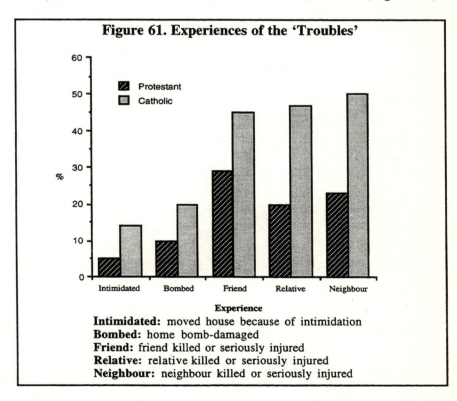

Figure 61. Experiences of the 'Troubles'

Intimidated: moved house because of intimidation
Bombed: home bomb-damaged
Friend: friend killed or seriously injured
Relative: relative killed or seriously injured
Neighbour: neighbour killed or seriously injured

Furthermore, they are twice as likely to have had a friend, relative or neighbour killed or seriously injured (although where these events occurred is unclear). Avoidance of future risk may be a major factor, therefore, in opting for the security of the segregated cluster. It might further be noted that proximity to the neighbourhood church, priests' house, school(s) and community centre appears to be an attraction for Catholics; this encourages additional spatial-social cohesion. The Catholic Church is, and is seen to be, a visible as well as a social and spiritual symbol of locality based community. This image may explain why almost three quarters of Protestant churchgoers see the Catholic community as united, although fewer than half the Catholics see themselves in this way. In turn, two thirds of them think of Protestants as being a united community although the Protestant churches do not provide the same local focus at neighbourhood level, given the distribution of churchgoers over several denominations and their attendance at geographically dispersed churches.

Finally, a word on perceptions of recent neighbourhood change. As Figure 62 shows, the majority of both groups, just over 50% of Protestants and 60% of Catholics, regard their neighbourhoods as having more or less the same religious composition as five years ago. Where change is perceived to have taken place, it is generally thought to be unidirectional. There is a convergence of opinion on the increasingly Catholic complexion of neighbourhoods; over one-third of both Catholic and Protestant churchgoers perceive that their neighbourhoods have been getting more Catholic over the last five years. On the other hand, few record any sense of their local area becoming more Protestant. The perception of neighbourhood composition, however, has to be interpreted with some caution; the perceived scale of in-movement of the 'other' group into a neighbourhood may depend on feelings of heightened threat. Furthermore, different Catholic and Protestant views of what constitutes mixing may also exist. Whatever, there is little doubt that where change has occurred it has normally been to increase the Catholic component, a pattern observed of minorities in other ethnically divided societies.

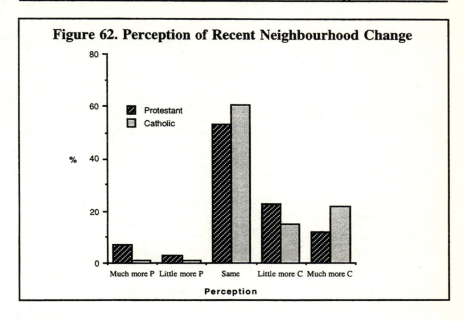

Figure 62. Perception of Recent Neighbourhood Change

Them And Us?

Considering these patterns of residential segregation and the behaviours and attitudes associated with the two groups, it is appropriate at this point to return to the church arena itself and to seek to determine the attitudes of churchgoers towards ecumenical affairs and cross-community interaction more generally.

Taken overall, churchgoers report a very considerable willingness to support closer links between the Protestant and Catholic churches. Nearly half of both Catholic and Protestant churchgoers indicate that the churches should aim for greater religious and social cooperation, although not for church unity. Beyond this, however, attitudes seem to diverge. Almost all other Catholics (47%) believe that the churches 'should aim for unity,' whereas this objective is favoured by only 10% of Protestants. Of the remaining Protestant churchgoers 34% advocate greater social interaction only, while 9% are opposed to any cooperation whatsoever. Catholic advocacy of church unity, of course, must be interpreted with a little care for, as has already been pointed out (Chapter 2), highly orthodox Catholics may well conceive of unity as a return of 'separated brethren' to the one true church.

What, then, of actual interaction? Given these attitudes, it is understandable that 44% of Protestants report having attended an ecumenical service of Protestants and Catholics. What is less obvious, at least on the surface, is the fact that only 50% of Catholics have participated in such ventures, notwithstanding the overwhelming support for interaction reported above. Their reticence, however, might well be a consequence of a lack of Catholic opportunity, given the religious geography of the city, to engage in such services. This suggestion would seem to be supported in part by the fact that 78% of churchgoing Catholics are willing to take part in a joint service of worship with the Church of Ireland,[3] even though the opportunity to do so may be limited. What we should note, however, is the highly selective nature of Catholic ecumenism; our findings register a marked decline in willingness among Catholics, across the Protestant denominational range, to take part in joint services dropping from the already noted 78% for Church of Ireland to 48% for Presbyterian and to only 11% for Free Presbyterian.

The support, albeit qualified, that churchgoers seem to give to ecumenical ventures, however, evidently does not translate into widespread direct personal involvement in cross-community organisations. Less than one in five churchgoing Protestants and Catholics report active involvement in such activities. And yet some two thirds of both groups express the view that the churches should be 'much more active' in 'trying to improve relations between the communities in Northern Ireland.' In keeping with this finding is the fact that 67% of Protestants and 76% of Catholics want sermons to deal with social and economic problems in Northern Ireland on at least some occasions. Both groups, however, seem less enthusiastic about

---

3. This affinity is also registered in the fact that the Church of Ireland is perceived by Catholics as, by far, the theologically closest Protestant denomination.

sermons directly addressing Northern Ireland's political problems with just over half expressing their support. This latter finding is difficult to explain, given the substantial expressed support for efforts at community reconciliation. But it may be the case that, for a large minority, such sermons reflect the direct politicisation of religious faith and the erosion of the church-state distinction. Some support for this interpretation may be had from the fact that it is the most theologically conservative Protestants and Catholics who are least in favour of sermons directly addressing domestic political questions.

And what about attitudes to cross-community mixing more generally? Regardless of attitudinal expressions, the actual mixing of Catholics and Protestants on a social and political basis is immediate in its impact. At the very least it provides the environment in which an opportunity for interaction is present. In time such interaction may have structural implications for relationships between the two groups. However, mixing does not mean integration, a matter frequently overlooked.

Attitudes to cross-community mixing can vary depending on the level of social intimacy involved and the more socially distant the links, as in the workplace, the happier people are with them. Catholics and Protestants in Belfast are no different to other social groups in this respect and, what is more, they are generally in agreement as regards the distance they wish to keep from one another. A range of expressions of social exclusivity is recorded in Figure 63.

Looking first at social openness in respect of marriage partners, it is clear that both Protestants and Catholics strongly favour endogamous relationships. However, where mixing is approved of Catholics are less hesitant to enter into such alliances. But however reticent Catholics are to enter a mixed marriage (for no more than a quarter of them would be happy to marry a Protestant) opposition to such marriages from Protestant churchgoers is much stronger; only 14% find inter-church marriage acceptable. What is notable, moreover, is that for both Protestants and Catholics an inter-racial marriage is preferable to marrying a Northern Ireland partner of the other religion.

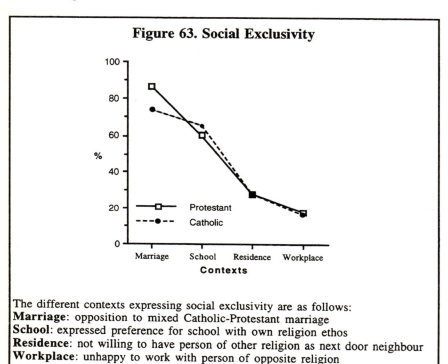

Figure 63. Social Exclusivity

The different contexts expressing social exclusivity are as follows:
Marriage: opposition to mixed Catholic-Protestant marriage
School: expressed preference for school with own religion ethos
Residence: not willing to have person of other religion as next door neighbour
Workplace: unhappy to work with person of opposite religion

Such attitudes to mixed marriages are likely to be reflected in views on the bringing up of children and, in particular, with respect to their schooling (see Figure 64). Although Protestants are a little happier than Catholics to have their children educated alongside Catholic children, what is clear is that there is a preference expressed by nearly two thirds of both Protestants and Catholics for religious exclusivity in the ethos of their schools. As far as schooling is concerned, then, some would argue that there is a legitimate doctrinal resistance to mixing exhibited by both religious groups, although others would claim that here we again find evidence of a deep seated unwillingness to take practical steps towards community reconciliation. Notwithstanding these views, however, there is almost unanimous support on all sides for children to work together on cross-community school projects. In spite of this, given the neighbourhood impact of schools, the homogenising effect on Belfast neighbourhoods of exclusivity in schooling should be noted.

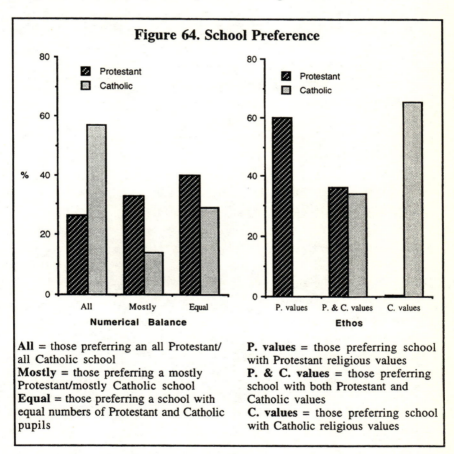

Figure 64. School Preference

All = those preferring an all Protestant/all Catholic school
Mostly = those preferring a mostly Protestant/mostly Catholic school
Equal = those preferring a school with equal numbers of Protestant and Catholic pupils

P. values = those preferring school with Protestant religious values
P. & C. values = those preferring school with both Protestant and Catholic values
C. values = those preferring school with Catholic religious values

Of undoubted and very considerable importance in cross-community terms are the social contacts made in the residential arena. It is within the worlds that they inhabit, and in which they experience life on a day to day basis, that an individual's social and political attitudes and aspirations are most likely to be formed and where the processes of social reproduction operate most effectively.

However willing Catholic and Protestant churchgoers are to work alongside one another, nearly a third of both groups still have reservations about having a neighbour of the other religion. Given the residential histories of the majority of Belfast churchgoers, regardless of their present residential environment, these reactions are not unexpected. Nonetheless, just over 70% of both Catholics and Protestants would be happy to have a neighbour of 'the other sort'; this figure is 30 percentage points higher than preferences expressed by both groups for residing in areas of more or less equal numbers of Catholics and Protestants. Looked at another way, however, it is just marginally higher than the 65% of Catholics who claim that they would like to live in a generally mixed area (mostly Catholic or having about equal numbers of both religious groups) but it seems at odds with the high level of Protestant preference expressed for such a mixed area (85%). It might be said, then, that while Catholics are more concerned about neighbourhood composition, Protestants are more sensitive about neighbours. At the same time, levels of tolerance for individuals, it seems, are considerable higher than for religiously-different groups.

It is worth exploring the impact that residential environment might have on subsequent residential preferences. If Belfast churchgoers are to be believed, the difference between those from mixed and those from totally segregated neighbourhoods is striking; those living where Protestants and Catholics are more or less equally mixed convey far greater acceptance of having a neighbour of 'the other sort' than their totally segregated co-religionists especially those from all-Protestant neighbourhoods. Even so, over half of them, as well as a third from totally segregated Catholic areas, would be happy to live beside someone from the other community. Whilst this should be taken into consideration in future planning to increase opportunities for residential mixing, looked at overall, both groups are a shade conservative in such matters. However, the neighbourhoods in which the ethnically conservative churchgoers reside are worth noting. As far as Catholics are concerned, few of those who adopt a conservative stance on matters of ethnic mixing reside in the most mixed situations (6% as compared to 68% in the totally segregated areas). As for Protestants, the difference between residential environments is still evident even if less pronounced (3 out of 10 conservatives are in mixed and 7 out of 10 in totally segregated areas). It is plausible to suggest that the differing residential environments with their differing religious, social and political underpinnings and their different levels of community cohesiveness may play a not insignificant role in the reproduction of attitudes towards members of 'the other community' and to the geography of Belfast.

Identity

Regardless of the substantial interest in cross-community links in some quarters, when it comes to the question of identity and to the constitutional future of Northern Ireland there is little agreement between Catholics and Protestants and only a little disagreement within each group (see Figure 65). In the first place, in a state where an understanding of the fundamental conflict over identity is imperative, how people describe themselves is significant. What is certain is that Protestants do not think of themselves as Irish (a mere 2%), although there is considerable group ambivalence as to a more positive identity; 4 out of 10 think of themselves as British and nearly the same number emphasise their Ulster dimension. What little support there is for a Northern Irish label (13%) comes from the residentially mixed areas.

As for Catholics, it is abundantly clear that, just as no more than 2% of Protestants consider themselves to be Irish, no more than 2% of Catholics regard themselves to be British. Instead, the overwhelming majority consider that their identity lies in some form of Irishness; 7 out of 10 describe themselves unequivocally as Irish and a further 2 out of 10 as Northern Irish.

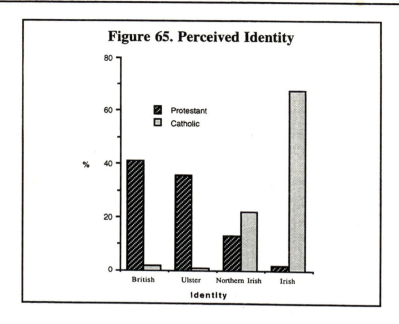

Figure 65. Perceived Identity

This conflict over national identity extends to the terms in which Belfast churchgoers describe the place to which they belong. Protestants identify with 'Northern Ireland' (over 80% as compared to just under half of Catholics). The remaining Protestants consider that they belong to 'Ulster', a term almost totally absent from the terminology of Catholic place identity. Instead the majority of Catholics perceive the place where they live in the context of Ireland as a whole. Moreover, this is reflected in the strong attraction that the Republic of Ireland holds as a favourite migration destination for Catholics in contrast to Protestants (36% and 2% respectively). It is no surprise, then, that the favoured out migration flow for Protestants is to a part of Great Britain, Scotland (39%), which is favoured by only 3% of Catholics.

The deep-seated, if very different, Protestant and Catholic feelings about self-understanding and self-determination conveyed by these expressions of national and place identity are of more practical significance when reflected in political terms. So far as matters of party preference is concerned (see Figure 66) there is a broad band of support from half of Protestant churchgoers for the middle-of-

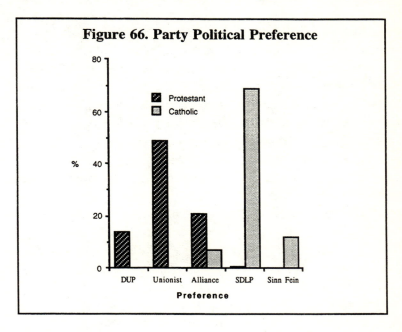

Figure 66. Party Political Preference

the-road Unionist party. Another 14% support the Democratic Unionist Party, a party attracting most of its support from the smaller theologically conservative denominations especially the Free Presbyterians. The little overlap that exists politically between Protestants and Catholics lies in support for the Alliance party with its cross-community if unionist philosophies. However, whilst one fifth of Protestants identify with it, only 7% of Catholics considered that it matched most closely with their aspirations. As for the main body of Catholic churchgoers, they are strongly in agreement that the SDLP comes closest to expressing their political views. This party enjoys almost 70% of Catholic support and, in contrast to the parties supported by Protestants, sees the future of Northern Ireland in an all-Ireland context. So also does Sinn Fein, the Republican party, which attracts 12% of Catholic support.

Differing attitudes towards the security situation in Northern Ireland further attest to deep-seated ideological differences between Protestant and Catholic churchgoers. The former are decidedly more likely to believe that dealing with the security situation here should be left *entirely* to the security forces. This stance is adopted by 82% of Protestant churchgoers, compared with only 38% of churchgoing Catholics. To put it another way, four out of five churchgoing Protestants have faith in the security structures of the state; nearly two thirds of churchgoing Catholics do not.

One final indication of a 'them-and-us' *mentalité* manifests itself in attitudes to the question of fairness in Northern Ireland society. Each group overwhelmingly perceives that 'the other' community is fairly treated these days. What is significantly different however, are feelings about one's own group. While only a quarter of Protestant churchgoers express the opinion that Protestants do not get a fair deal, the figure jumps dramatically to three quarters of Catholic churchgoers believing that Catholics are not fairly treated. This dissonance in attitudes to societal equity evidently displays a substantial degree of alienation by the Catholic community, though (compared with the findings of our 1983 survey of Protestant churchgoers) there undoubtedly is an increased sense of Protestant alienation. For example, while in 1983 less than a quarter of supporters of the Democratic Unionist Party expressed the view that Protestants were not getting a fair deal, the figure has now jumped to half; with Official Unionists it has shifted from 13% to 26%.[4]

The Future Of Northern Ireland

Whatever slight differences exist among Catholics and among Protestants on matters of identity concerning nationality, place and political partisanship, the overwhelming differences between the two communities are crystal clear. And when it comes to attitudes to the

---

4. It is not possible to make a similar comparison for Catholic churchgoers, since the 1983 survey only covered Protestants.

constitutional future of Northern Ireland the differences are, indeed, profound. There is an almost universal conviction among Protestant churchgoers (89%) that the future of Northern Ireland should be as part of the United Kingdom rather than in an all-Ireland framework or as an independent state (see Figure 67). This does not mean that

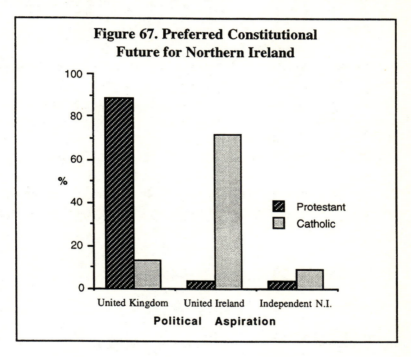

Protestants were united in their reason for opposing a United Ireland; around 70% agreed, in almost equal proportions, on either their fear of the power of the Catholic Church in such a situation or else their wish to retain a British identity. The sense of psychological unease that surrounds these aspirations can be appreciated when it is realised that some four out of every five Protestant churchgoers in Belfast believe that at some time in the future 'more than half the population in Northern Ireland will be Catholic.' What is more, some 70% of these churchgoers are convinced that this demographic shift will occur within the next thirty years.

At odds with the voice of the Protestant city, support for a United Ireland among over 70% of Catholic churchgoers outweighs any other option. Moreover, two-thirds agree that, above all else, an all-Ireland framework would give them a chance to express their Irish identity. The fact that 85% of Catholic churchgoers believe that there will be a Catholic majority in Northern Ireland—and for almost 80% of these that this circumstance will occur within thirty years—indicates considerable psychological confidence.

The opposition of Protestants to a United Ireland clearly springs from an uneasiness about their religious identity and its future security; indeed for some (24%) their religious convictions are tied fast to the territory of Northern Ireland. Even this degree of Protestant linking of religion to territory is generally at odds with a Catholic outlook. However, the intimate connections between religious conviction, political identity and territory highlight the deep lines of rupture between 'the two traditions' in Northern Ireland but at the same time draw attention to the complexities hidden in such a seemingly simple interpretation.

Conclusion

There are good grounds, then, for querying the stereotypical perceptions of Catholics and Protestants in Belfast as discrete monolithic groups. Indeed, as we have seen, a remarkable degree of convergence exists in their characteristics and convictions. In general, they are very similar in terms of gender balance, age profile, and social class composition. Churchgoing also tends to be a female, middle-aged to elderly concern rather than one which attracts young Protestants and Catholics today; nevertheless, when present, young Protestants display a conservatism which contrasts markedly with the more liberal, less orthodox, outlook of young Catholic churchgoers. The implications of this for the future are likely to be considerable. If present trends continue it seems that churchgoing Protestantism is likely to become more theologically conservative in outlook, while the Catholic churchgoing community may increasingly experience the inroads of secularization or be subject to a growing theological liberalism. Finally, we note that organised religion does not attract the working classes in the same proportions as it does the middle classes, and few unemployed are among the churchgoing ranks, whether Protestant or Catholic.

Overall, Belfast's churchgoers are conservative, committed to traditional doctrinal stances, and ardent in devotional practice, even if Protestants are more Bible-centred and conversionist, while Catholics could be described as a community of faith. In spite of that, there is a sameness in their ethical codes, especially in respect of sexual matters; they even agree on the circumstances under which abortion might be legally acceptable, although Catholics are a shade more pro-life. Catholics are also less disciplinarian and less sabbatarian than Protestants and are more likely to remain with the religion of their birth.

As for attitudes to one another, it is clear that—taken overall—neither group of churchgoers is averse to ecumenical mixing. However, when it comes to other types of mixing, what they share is a strong pull towards group exclusiveness—in marriage, schooling and in housing. Whether this reflects very high levels of residential segregation in their respective upbringings, or whether it is something deeper is not clear. What is certain is that a deep chasm exists in respect of identity, whether national or political, and in their respective sense of place. Catholics feel strongly Irish as compared to tiny numbers of Protestants and, in turn, few Catholic churchgoers express a sense of being British. Not unexpectedly, then, the gap between their respective visions of the future is great. Most Protestants see their future within a United Kingdom context, while most Catholics envisage it within an all-Ireland framework. A small number of Protestant churchgoers add a further religious dimension which is rooted in their sense of need for territorial recognition.

Too often the divergence of behaviour and attitude is emphasised without addressing the array of convergent characteristics shown by Catholics and Protestants. Given that many of these similarities are located in religious experience, it might well be profitable to listen to the view shared by both churchgoing traditions, namely, that the churches ought to be more active in Northern Ireland affairs.

V

Afterword

If, as Wittgenstein would have put it, the limits of our language are the limits of our world, then how we conceive of, and talk about, ourselves and about others is of the utmost importance. We all inherit sets of labels and attendant concepts which we use to understand the world we live in and our place within it. These vocabularies are, at once, enabling and constraining, clarifying and obfuscating. On the one hand, they provide a means of making sense of who we are, how we act, and where we live. On the other, they can stultify imagination, suppress creativity, and circumscribe reality.

The people of Northern Ireland have lived with the power of language—for good or ill. Labelling, while foundational to the maintenance of identity, can too easily induce the ideological fixity which underpins intransigence. The dichotomised rhetoric of two traditions, two communities, and two identities, encapsulated as they are in the labels 'Catholic' and 'Protestant', is so much part of conventional wisdom that it seems to be inviolate, beyond questioning. It cannot be denied that there is a range of key political issues on which Protestants and Catholics are diametrically opposed; on matters of national identity, political partisanship and constitutional aspiration the gap is wide indeed. However, underlying political equifinality—the final objectives of constitutional aspiration—is a continuum of social and political motivations and strategies that runs from the exclusionist to the inclusionist. Thus, to subsume every aspect of social life and cultural identity under the bi-polar rubric of constitutional antithesis is to fall captive to a political reductionism whose status is highly contestable.

The deceptive simplicity of the labels 'Protestant' and 'Catholic' itself illustrates this. In the first place, despite the apparently religious connotations of these terms, they are typically invested with almost exclusively political meaning. However, our survey clearly demonstrates that religion matters in Belfast and that the religious spaces that dot the urban landscape are of immense significance even though they remain largely *terrae incognitae* to the eye of much scholarship and political commentary. Furthermore, it is clear that these Catholic and Protestant spaces are themselves far from monochrome. Rather they constitute a diverse array of sites and social spaces within which culture is differentially reproduced.

The findings we have presented in this study illustrate something of the complexities of life in Northern Ireland. On issues of religious belief and practice, public and private morality, cross-community relations and experience, and motivations for political stance, we have discerned significant variation *within* each of the two sets of churchgoers—Catholics and Protestants. For both, these variations correlate particularly with individual religious conviction, with age and with dimensions of social class, and—for Protestants—with denominational affiliation. This lack of internal cohesiveness also points to the fact that there may well be much in common between groups of Catholics and Protestants who share similar moral values, cultural aspirations and social outlooks, thereby straddling the 'traditional' divide, albeit at times within narrow ambits. The implications of this state of affairs for our use of language and for the retention of a two-label mentality are considerable. Diversity may defy collective labelling, but collective labelling, in turn, suppresses diversity and encourages stereotyping. Consequently, such stereotypical portrayal of two traditions in Northern Ireland—'them and us'—fails, we believe, to do justice to reality, however analytically convenient or politically expedient such a rudimentary dualistic taxonomy may appear to be.

Appendices

I   Methodology
II   Protestant Questionnaire
III   Catholic Questionnaire
IV   Morality Scales

Appendix I

Methodology

In order to fulfil the objectives of the project the following research strategy was devised and, subsequently, put into operation.

Selection of Survey Areas
The number of areas selected was sufficient to ensure a range of socio-spatial contexts within which individual congregations could be examined. Criteria used to differentiate were social class characteristics, religious affiliation (Catholic/Protestant), ethnic pressure edges, inner city and suburbs. In addition, note was taken of areas surveyed previously in 1983, so that temporal comparison would be possible for certain issues. The following locations were identified: University (Un), Outer Falls (OF), Inner Falls (IF), Inner North (IN), Shankill (Sk), Outer North (ON), East Belfast (EB).

Selection of Survey Sites
Having delimited the study areas, the constituent congregational 'sites' were identified. This provided, for survey purposes, a list of individual congregations most of which were affiliated with larger denominational groupings. Initially, 77 sites were identified. Clergy were contacted to ascertain if they would be willing to participate in the project. Subsequently, it transpired that a number of institutions did not wish to be included in the project and a number of additional sites were incorporated to provide greater balance and enlarge coverage. Overall 81 churches agreed to be surveyed (see Table 18).

Clergy interviews took place over the period of March—May 1993. The interviews were guided by schedules, one for Catholic and one for Protestant clergy. The development of the schedules themselves involved input from members of the Religious Advisory Panel set up to represent a wide range of church/theological backgrounds. The interviews were designed to provide information on the congregational histories, current activities, the 'congregational mind,' attendance numbers, the characteristics of the area within which the church is located and the personal background and attitudes of the priest or minister. Clergy were also asked to fill in a questionnaire, the same as that administered to the church attenders, which would allow comparison with the laity. Overall, 47 Protestant clergy and 25 Catholic clergy completed questionnaires.

Table 18. Denomination by Area

	Un	OF	IF	IN	Sk	ON	EB	Total
Catholic	1	6	6	3	0	3	2	**21**
Church of Ireland	2	1	0	3	1	2	2	**11**
Presbyterian	1	1	0	2	1	4	2	**11**
Methodist	1	1	1	0	1	2	2	**8**
Baptist	1	0	0	2	0	0	4	**7**
Pentecostal	0	0	0	0	3	2	1	**6**
Brethren	1	0	0	1	0	1	0	**3**
Free Presbyterian	1	0	0	1	0	0	2	**4**
Evangelical Pres	1	0	0	1	0	0	0	**2**
Congregational	0	0	0	0	1	0	1	**2**
Others	3	0	0	0	0	0	3	**6**
Total	**12**	**9**	**7**	**13**	**7**	**14**	**19**	**81**

Sample Size Determination

The sampling populations were those attending individual 'services'—each mass at the Catholic churches and morning service at the Protestant churches. Initially a target of +/- 10% at a confidence level of 95% was set. This yielded an estimated sample size of around 10,000. However the feedback from the denominations suggested that, at least in certain situations, response rates might be low. In consequence, the sample target was changed to +/- 5% at 95%. This indicated a sample size of 22,000. In terms of production, distribution and collection the marginal costs involved in this increase in sample size were small. It should be noted that while sample size determination was based on the sample population of churchgoers at each sample site, most subsequent analysis is for aggregations of these sites (denominations, areas) or aggregations of respondents (based on social class, gender, age, theological position etc.). Thus confidence limits for much of our analysis is significantly tighter than +/- 10%.

Questionnaire Design and Development

Two parallel questionnaires were designed, one for use in Catholic churches, the other in Protestant. Both questionnaires share many common questions and almost all the same topics were covered. However, in some cases, the nature of specific questions had to be adapted to suit each particular 'constituency'. Questionnaires were designed to obtain information about the following:

>   Personal characteristics of the respondent
>   Religious practice and belief
>   Moral and social issues
>   Neighbourhood characteristics
>   Politics

Questionnaire development involved a series of steps. Background reading included examination of previous surveys. Relevant publications on the sociology of religion and religion in Ireland were reviewed and a number of earlier surveys of religious attitudes were consulted with a view to making later comparisons. Of particular importance was the review of the 1983 survey of Protestant Churchgoers.

Drafts of the questionnaire were sent to the Religious Advisory Panel for comment. The following participated in consultation: Aidan Burns, Pauline Coll, Rev. Dr. John Dunlop, Dr. Tom Gardiner, Dr. Tom Kirk, Pamela Lockie, Right Rev. Monsignor Ambrose Macaulay, Sister Christina O'Neill, Rev. Dr. Ian Paisley, Patrick Roche, Dr. David Stevens and Canon Edgar Turner.

Drafts were also sent to participating clergy and comments were received in July - August 1993. In addition to this, consultations with the Bishop of Down and Connor took place on several occasions regarding the Catholic questionnaire and a draft was discussed at a specially convened meeting of Catholic clergy. Moreover, individual questions and groups of questions were piloted as part of the process.

Once the consultation process had finished and comments had been brought together, the final versions of Questionnaires were agreed (see Appendices II and III). The questionnaires consisted of four parts as follows:

>   Part 1   Demographics
>   Part 2   Religious Views
>   Part 3   Neighbourhood
>   Part 4   Life and Society in Northern Ireland

Distribution and Collection of Questionnaires

Survey Sunday was set for October 31st 1993. Given the general sensitivity of the subject matter of our questionnaire and its particular sensitivity in the context of Northern Ireland, it was of paramount importance that the total anonymity of our respondents be maintained. This requirement would be most fully met by having the questionnaire distributed by each minister/priest, and, much more importantly, by having the completed questionnaires returned via him/her in a sealed unmarked envelope. There were, besides, other advantages in this method. Firstly, it allowed the church for each respondent to be identified. Secondly, it would produce, with ministerial encouragement, a higher return than might be expected from more conventional distribution means (for instance postal surveys). Thirdly, it did not require a full scale interviewing team, which, in any case, would have subverted the requirement of total confidentiality and anonymity. The churches were telephoned, followed by a letter notifying the Survey date. Appropriate numbers of questionnaires for each church were placed in labelled and unsealed envelopes. Questionnaire Distribution Guidelines were presented to priests and ministers to help in distribution. Questionnaires were to be given to attenders on the specified Sunday on a systematic basis, the fraction in each instance dependent upon the particular sampling requirement applying to the church concerned. Collection boxes for questionnaire returns were prepared and delivered to survey sites.

The Shankill bombing occurred on Saturday 23rd October and the Greysteel shooting on Saturday 30th October. In consequence, we moved Survey Sunday to November 21st. Given these circumstances, together with local church programmes, five churches distributed the questionnaire on Sunday October 24th and six went ahead, as originally arranged, on October 31st. It should be noted that these dates indicate when the questionnaires were *given* to respondents. The questionnaires could have been filled out any time between receipt and return (a period for each church of some two to three weeks). The large majority of churches (including all Catholic churches) distributed the questionnaire on Sunday, November 21st.

The completed questionnaires were collected from the churches approximately three weeks after distribution.

Response

A total of 5,255 completed questionnaires was obtained. This total was composed of 3,176 Catholic returns, 2,054 Protestant returns and 25 from the Society of Friends. Although the questionnaires were distributed to and collected from individual churches, analysis was not intended to be, and was not conducted at *this* scale. Instead, our intention has been to analyse our data at the level of a variety of aggregations, such as denominational affiliation and geographical area, and other characteristics to be determined from scrutinising the returns themselves (such as theological viewpoint, political persuasion and socio-economic class). Table 18 shows the response for the two main categories (Catholic and Protestant) and Table 19 for the individual denominations. The table also indicates the number of returns required to achieve a confidence level of +/- 5% at 95%.

Table 18. Overall Returns

	Total Returns	95% +/-5%	Response Rate%
Catholic	3,176	381	21
Protestant	2,054	369	38
Quakers	25	25	93

Table 19. Returns by Protestant Denomination

	Total Returns	95% +/-5%	Response Rate%
Presbyterian	456	325	37
Church of Ireland	434	290	43
Methodist	337	290	38
Minor	*486*	*321*	*34*
Baptist	206	268	31
Brethren	51	68	61
Evangelical Presbyterian	44	103	33
Free Presbyterian	103	232	30
Congregational	82	155	38
Others	*343*	*337*	*42*
Non-Subscribing Presbyterian	23	40	51
Independent Evangelical	44	168	30
Moravian	18	43	56
Pentecostal	195	318	46
Charismatic Fellowship	63	217	39

It will be seen that the required level has been attained for the major denominations individually. It has also been attained for the minor denominations as a group, though not for the individual components. A third set of 'denominations' has been listed, though in most cases these are, in fact, individual/independent churches. Here again the +/- 5% at 95 % accuracy has been attained for the aggregate of these units. Finally the necessary confidence level has been attained for the Quakers. (We have agreed with the Society of Friends that they should not be categorised as Catholic or Protestant).

It will be noted that the Catholic response (treated as a single denominational return) is much greater than the denominational level requirement. Indeed, the Catholic return is such that we have obtained a response adequate to meet the requirements of +/- 10% at 99% for all but two of the individual Catholic *parishes*. This degree of accuracy was set because of the central importance of the Catholic data in our overall study design, where we planned to examine variation within the Catholic church-going community in a fairly detailed fashion.

When we turn to the second aggregation, that for the seven sampling areas (Table 20), we find that the +/- 5% at 95% confidence level is attained in all instances.

Table 20. Returns by Area

	Total Returns	95% +/-5%	Response Rate%
Area 1 : University	600	354	28
Area 2 : Outer Falls	1083	375	23
Area 3 : Inner Falls	1032	372	24
Area 4 : Inner North	672	369	23
Area 5 : Shankill	271	254	43
Area 6 : Outer North	726	364	30
Area 7 : East Belfast	850	357	30
Total	5234		26

NB There were also 21 questionnaires with no area information available due to the fact that they were mailed back to us directly. In addition to the 5,255 churchgoer responses, we also have to hand 70 responses from the clergy and lay leaders of the churches surveyed.

Coding and Computer Analysis

The coding and computer analysis of the questionnaire responses involved several stages, thus:

1. Checking and editing of questionnaires;
2. Development of coding frame for open-ended questions;
3. Development of two coding manuals (Catholic and Protestant questionnaires);
4. Formation and training of coding team;
5. Coding;
6. Transfer of codes to data sheets (incorporating coding accuracy checks);
7. Data entry and Verification to the Queen's University VAX9000 Mainframe Computer;
8. Creation of SPSS files;
9. Cleaning of files.

Preliminary computer analysis of the data was by SPSS statistical package involving frequency counts on each variable for all cases.

Check on Churchgoers' Sample Reliability

It was decided that it would be useful to have a cross-check on the representativeness of our response. Although we obtained (and in many instances exceeded) the sample sizes required for the main aggregations (denomination and area), there is the risk that we have, nonetheless, obtained a biased return—do the people who *did not* return their questionnaires have the same characteristics as those *who did*? We cannot check on many aspects of our response, but it is possible to examine some of the demographic dimensions. This has been done by employing data from the Northern Ireland Continuous Household Survey (CHS).[1]

Method

1. Data were obtained on CHS respondents who claimed that they attended church at least once a week.

2. The CHS data were obtained for persons over 18 years of age resident in the Belfast District Council area. Our survey sites were all located within the Belfast District Council area.

---

1. We are grateful to Dr. Kevin Sweeney and Ms. Eilish Murtagh at the Policy Planning and Research Unit, Department of Finance and Personnel, Government of Northern Ireland, for supplying special tabulations from the CHS files.

3. To maximise the reliability of the Belfast District Council CHS subset, the CHS returns were aggregated for the years 1987 through 1993 (6079 returns).

4. The CHS (frequent churchgoers) and the Belfast Churchgoers survey (BCG) responses were compared on three characteristics—age, sex and socio-economic group (see Tables 21, 22, 23). The results of these comparisons are given below:

Table 21. Age Profiles

Age	R. C.		Presb.		C. of I.		Meth.		Other Prot.	
	BCG	CHS	BCG	CHS	BCG	CHS	BCG	CHS	BCG	CHS
18-34	15%	33%	12%	20%	16%	13%	10%	16%	25%	28%
35-64	51%	47%	40%	34%	43%	46%	42%	45%	51%	47%
65+	34%	20%	48%	46%	42%	40%	48%	39%	24%	26%

Table 22. Sex Profiles

Sex	R. C.		Presb.		C. of I.		Meth.		Other Prot.	
	BCG	CHS	BCG	CHS	BCG	CHS	BCG	CHS	BCG	CHS
Male	40%	38%	44%	28%	34%	30%	34%	29%	48%	40%
Female	60%	62%	56%	72%	66%	70%	66%	71%	52%	60%

Table 23. Socio-Economic Profiles

Occupation	R. C.		Presby.		C. of I.		Other Prot.[2]	
	BCG	CHS	BCG	CHS	BCG	CHS	BCG	CHS
Non-Manual	49%	38%	73%	55%	66%	43%	61%	46%
Manual	48%	62%	27%	45%	34%	57%	39%	54%

2. The 'Other Protestant' category in Table 23 contains the Methodist Denomination.

The following observations can be made:

1. Age: The youngest age category (18-34) is underrepresented in the Catholic response. This is also true, though to a lesser extent, for Presbyterians. Otherwise there is a reasonable CHS/BCG correspondence.

2. Sex: A good fit in male/female proportions for all groups except the Presbyterians, where males appear to be over-represented.

3. Socio-economic groups: With all groupings those with 'non-manual' backgrounds are over-represented on BCG vis-à-vis CHS.

Comments

1. CHS is based on those resident in the Belfast District Council (BDC) area. BCG is based on those attending church in selected segments of the Belfast District Council area. Church-going 'commuters' from outside the BDC area (particularly in the case of Protestants) may well have contributed to churchgoers being more middle class than the proportions indicated in CHS.

2. Middle-class churchgoers may have been more likely to fill in and return lengthy self-completion questionnaires than would be the case with churchgoers from working class backgrounds.

3. It may be that our sample is *more* representative of frequent churchgoers than the CHS subset. Our respondents *had* to be fairly frequent churchgoers (to both collect and return the questionnaire); CHS respondents had only to tick a box on a questionnaire.

Weighting of the Protestant Response
The analysis of Protestant churchgoers has been carried out on two data files—the un-weighted and the weighted. The un-weighted file was employed for the 'Denominational' analysis and includes all returns received (2054). For all other analyses the weighted file has been used. Having obtained a somewhat variable response rate from the denominations (together with varying sample size requirements) it was considered desirable that the number of respondents should be weighted in order to make the overall response more fully representative of the areas surveyed. The weighting was carried out as follows:

1. A number of individual congregations were excluded. These comprised 6 congregations that lay outside the survey areas but which had been

included to numerically strengthen certain denominational returns. The Society of Friends was also excluded.

2. The response for each denomination was expressed as a percentage of all responses.

3. Employing estimated attendance figures (as provided by clergy) the attendance at each denomination was expressed as a percentage of the total attendance.

4. A weight was calculated for each denomination, the weight being the ratio *between* the percentage that the particular denomination's return was of the total return *and* the percentage that the particular denomination's attendance was of the total attendance (See Table 24).

Table 24. Weightings

Denomination	Returns	% BCG	Estimated Attendance	% Attendance	Weight	Weighted Returns
C. of Ireland	432	24.40	1177	19.16	0.79	341
Presby.	453	25.59	2098	34.16	1.33	602
Methodist	307	17.34	1027	16.72	0.96	295
Baptist	164	9.27	635	10.34	1.12	184
Brethren	51	2.88	83	1.35	.47	24
Ev. Presby.	44	2.49	140	2.28	.92	40
Fr. Presby.	42	2.37	86	1.4	.59	25
N.-S. Presby.	23	1.29	45	.73	.57	13
Congreg.	81	4.58	260	4.23	.92	75
Indep. Ev.	44	2.49	300	4.88	1.96*	(86) 44
Moravian	18	1.02	49	0.80	.78	14
Pentecostal	111	6.27	242	3.94	.63	70
All	1770	100	6142	100		1727

Note: * In this instance the weight obtained by the above method was not applied. Here (Independent Evangelical Church) a weight of 1 was used producing 44 returns rather than 86. The reason for this is that here we have a single congregation that is not part of any larger denomination.

Appendix II

Protestant Questionnaire

SURVEY OF BELFAST CHURCHGOERS 1993

Over the past number of years we have all seen changes in many aspects of life in Northern Ireland. At present we are carrying out a study of how churchgoing people feel about these changes.

Your church is in one of the areas that has been chosen to be part of the survey. A number of people from each church are being asked to help by answering our questionnaire, and we very much hope that you will be able to find time to take part. Most of the questions only require you to tick a box.

We can assure you that every answer will be treated in the strictest confidence. We don't know who you are; we only want to know what church you attend and what area you live in.

The results of this survey will be extremely valuable for understanding people's responses to many of the major changes that have been taking place in our society.

After filling in the questionnaire, please place it in the envelope provided, seal, and return to the box as instructed by your minister / pastor / leader.

Thank you.

Belfast Churchgoers Survey 1993
Department of Geography
The Queen's University of Belfast
Belfast, BT7 1NN

PART I

In this first part of the survey we want to ask you some general questions about yourself and your family.

1. Are you male or female? *(Please tick)*   Male ☐   Female ☐

2. Are you....? *(Please tick one box)*

    Single   Married   Separated   Divorced   Widowed   Other
    ☐   ☐   ☐   ☐   ☐   ☐

3. (a) Do you have children? *(Please tick)*   YES ☐   NO ☐

    (b) If YES, how many? *(Please tick one box)*

    1 ☐   2 ☐   3 ☐   4 ☐   5+ ☐

4. What age are you? *(Please tick one box)*

    17 and under   18-24   25-34   35-44   45-54   55-64   65 and over
    ☐   ☐   ☐   ☐   ☐   ☐   ☐

5. Is your home....? *(Please tick one box)*

    Rented from the Housing Executive   ☐
    Owner Occupied   ☐
    Other   ☐

6. What type of school / college did you last attend full time? *(Please tick one box)*

    Primary/Elementary   ☐   F.E. College/Technical College   ☐
    Secondary/Intermediate ☐   University/Poly/College of Education   ☐
    Grammar   ☐   Other *(please specify)*   ☐
    _____

7. (a) What was the home background in which **you were brought up**? *(Please tick **one** box)*

Professional	☐	Semi-Skilled Manual	☐
Managerial	☐	Unskilled Manual	☐
Skilled Manual	☐	Other *(please specify)*	☐
Clerical / Sales	☐	_____	

    (b) What is your **present** home background? *(Please tick **one** box)*

Professional	☐	Semi-Skilled Manual	☐
Managerial	☐	Unskilled Manual	☐
Skilled Manual	☐	Other *(please specify)*	☐
Clerical / Sales	☐	_____	

8. (a) Have you ever been employed? *(Please tick)*   YES ☐   NO ☐

    (b) If **YES**, please tell us what your occupation is (or was). Please describe the job as precisely as possible.

    _____

    (c) At present, are you....? *(please tick **one** box)*

Employed: Full time	☐	Student/Pupil	☐
Employed: Part time	☐	Permanently sick/Disabled	☐
Unemployed : Short term (1 yr or less)	☐	Y.T.P.	☐
Unemployed : Long term (1 yr+)	☐	Retired	☐
Looking after home / family	☐	Other	☐

9. (a) Are you the head of your household? *(Please tick)*   YES ☐   NO ☐

    (b) If **NO**, please describe what your head of household's occupation is (or was).

    _____

    Never had a job ☐

PART II

We would now like to ask you some questions about your religious views.

1. (a) What religious denomination do you belong to?
   _____

   (b) Have you always belonged to this denomination? *(please tick)*

          YES ☐   NO ☐

   (c) If your answer is NO, please give us the name of your previous denomination, if any?
   _____

2. (a) Which church do you attend at present?
   _____

   (b) How long have you been attending your present church? *(Please tick one box)*

   Less than 1 Year ☐   6-10 Years ☐
   1-5 Years ☐   More than 10 Years ☐

3. How do you normally get to church? *(Please tick one box)*

   Walk ☐   Church Bus ☐   Public Transport ☐   Car ☐   Other ☐

4. Do you hold or have you recently held any position of leadership either in your church or in any organization associated with it? *(Please tick)*

          YES ☐   NO ☐

   If your answer is YES, would you please tell us what position you hold or held?
   _____

5. (a) About how often do you go to Sunday Service? *(Please tick **one** box)*

Twice or more on a Sunday	☐	Several times a year	☐
Once a Sunday	☐	Once a year	☐
2-3 times a month	☐	Less than once a year	☐
Once a month	☐		

   (b) About how often do you go to...? *(Please tick **one** box)*

	Mid-week Service	Church Recreational Activities
Twice a week or more	☐	☐
Once a week	☐	☐
2-3 times a month	☐	☐
Once a month	☐	☐
Several times a year	☐	☐
Once a year	☐	☐
Less than once a year	☐	☐
Never	☐	☐

6. About how often do you pray in private? *(Please tick **one** box)*

Twice a day or more	☐	Sometimes but not regularly	☐
Once a day	☐	Rarely or only on special occasions	☐
Several times a week	☐	Never	☐
Once a week	☐		

7. About how often do you read the Bible in private? *(Please tick **one** box)*

Once a day or more	☐	Sometimes but not regularly	☐
Several times a week	☐	Rarely or only on special occasions	☐
Once a week	☐	Never	☐

8. Does your family join together in any of the following? *(Please tick **as many boxes as you require**)*

Grace / prayers at meal-times	☐	Praying	☐
Bible reading	☐	Going to church	☐

9. Could you tell us how firmly you believe in the following? *(Please tick one box for each)*

	Believe Firmly	Believe With Difficulty	Partly Believe/ Partly Reject	Unsure	Reject
(a)					
The Resurrection of Christ	☐	☐	☐	☐	☐
The Bible is the Word of God	☐	☐	☐	☐	☐
People can sin	☐	☐	☐	☐	☐
There is life after death	☐	☐	☐	☐	☐
There is a Heaven	☐	☐	☐	☐	☐
The Devil exists	☐	☐	☐	☐	☐
There is a Hell	☐	☐	☐	☐	☐
(b)					
Miracles of healing happen today	☐	☐	☐	☐	☐
Some people today have the gift of 'speaking in tongues'	☐	☐	☐	☐	☐

10. Which if any of the following statements **comes closest to** what you think makes someone a Christian? *(please tick one box)*

Being brought up as a member of a Christian family makes you a Christian ☐
Being brought up in a church makes you a Christian ☐
Regularly attending church services makes you a Christian ☐
Only a conversion experience of Jesus Christ as personal
    Saviour makes you a Christian ☐
All people who try to live their lives as Christ lived his are Christians ☐
Living in a Christian country makes you a Christian ☐
Believing in God makes you a Christian ☐
People who try to live moral and upright lives are Christians ☐

If none of these statements comes close to your view, would you please tell us what you think makes a person a Christian.

_____

11. Would you say that you have had a turning point in your life when you committed yourself to Christ? *(please tick)*

       YES ☐   NO ☐   Don't Know ☐

12. Which if any of the following, **comes closest to** what you believe about the Bible? *(please tick one box)*

What is written in the Bible is the Word of God and is completely □
without error
What is written in the Bible is the Word of God but it contains a few □
minor errors
The Bible contains many errors in matters of history and science, □
but it is none the less a statement of religious truth

If you feel that none of these statements comes close to your own view, would you please tell us in your own words what you believe about the Bible.

_____

13. Do you agree or disagree with this statement: "Every passage in the Bible should be taken literally (except where the Bible itself indicates otherwise)." *(Please tick one box)*

Strongly Agree   Agree   Disagree   StronglyDisagree   Don't Know
     □   □   □   □   □

14. Do you have a particular view of biblical prophecy about the Second Coming of Christ and the "last times"? *(please tick one box)*

YES □   NO □

If **YES**, please tell us in your own words what your views about this are?

_____

15. Which of these versions of Genesis ch.1 v. 26 would you prefer to hear read from the Bible in church? *(please tick one box)*

"Let us make **man** in our image"   □
or
"Let us make **humankind** in our image"   □

16. Do you agree with ordinary church members taking part in services in any of the following ways? *(please tick **one** box for each)*

	YES	NO
Officiating at Communion / Lord's Supper	☐	☐
Preaching regularly in church	☐	☐
Leading public prayer	☐	☐
Reading the scriptures in church	☐	☐

17. Do you approve or disapprove of a woman taking part in any of the following in your church? *(please tick **one** box for each)*

	Strongly Approve	Approve	Disapprove	Strongly Disapprove	Don't Know	Not Applicable
Being Treasurer of the church	☐	☐	☐	☐	☐	☐
Preaching sermons in church	☐	☐	☐	☐	☐	☐
Going as a missionary	☐	☐	☐	☐	☐	☐
Being the Pastor / Minister	☐	☐	☐	☐	☐	☐
Teaching a Sunday School class	☐	☐	☐	☐	☐	☐
Being an Elder	☐	☐	☐	☐	☐	☐

18. Do you agree or disagree with this statement? "It is more important to remain loyal to my own church than to my own convictions." (*Please tick **one** box*)

Strongly Agree	Agree	Disagree	StronglyDisagree	Don't Know
☐	☐	☐	☐	☐

19. Which other denomination do you think is **closest in doctrine** to your own?

_____

20. (a) Have you ever attended an Ecumenical Service of Protestants and Catholics? (*Please tick*)

        YES ☐   NO ☐

(b) With which of the following would you be happy to take part in a joint service of worship? *(Please tick **as many** boxes as you require)*

Church of Ireland	☐	Methodist	☐
Free Presbyterian	☐	Brethren	☐
Congregational	☐	Presbyterian	☐
Evangelical Presbyterian	☐	Quaker	☐
Pentecostal	☐	Baptist	☐
Reformed Presbyterian	☐	Salvation Army	☐
Non-Subscribing Presbyterian	☐	Catholic	☐

None Of These ☐

21. Which of the following statements comes closest to what you feel about future relations between the Protestant and Catholic churches? *(please tick **one** box)*

They should aim for unity ☐

They should not aim for unity but for greater co-operation in religious and social matters ☐

They should not aim for unity but for greater co-operation in social matters only ☐

They should not aim for unity nor for greater co-operation on anything ☐

22. How active do you think the churches should be in trying to improve relations between the communities in Northern Ireland? *(please tick **one** box)*

Much more active than now	☐	A little less active than now	☐
A little more active than now	☐	Much less active than now	☐
About the same as now	☐	Don't Know	☐

23. Are you, or have you been, actively involved in cross-community organizations? *(please tick **one** box)*

YES ☐   NO ☐

If **YES**, which? _____

24. (a) Do you agree or disagree with these statements: "Sermons should deal with Northern Ireland's social and economic problems on at least some occasions." *(Please tick **one** box)*

Strongly Agree	Agree	Disagree	Strongly Disagree	Don't Know
☐	☐	☐	☐	☐

(b) "Sermons should deal with Northern Ireland's political problems on at least some occasions." *(Please tick **one** box)*

Strongly Agree	Agree	Disagree	Strongly Disagree	Don't Know
☐	☐	☐	☐	☐

25. What do you think about the following **moral** issues: *(please tick **one** box for each)*

	Always Wrong	Generally Wrong	Depends	Generally Right	Always Right
Sex before marriage	☐	☐	☐	☐	☐
Living together outside marriage	☐	☐	☐	☐	☐
Abortion	☐	☐	☐	☐	☐
Homosexual Practice	☐	☐	☐	☐	☐

26. Are there ever any circumstances in which you think divorce is acceptable? *(Please tick **as many** boxes as you require)*

Under no circumstances	☐	When desertion occurs	☐
When adultery is committed	☐	When the partners are not suited	☐
When physical violence occurs	☐	When the marriage breaks down	☐
When mental cruelty occurs	☐		

Other *(please specify)* _____

27. Are there ever any circumstances in which abortion should be **legally** available? *(Please tick **as many** boxes as you require)*

When the couple do not want   ☐   No, not in any circumstances   ☐
another child

When it is likely that the child will be   ☐   When the mother-to-be is too   ☐
born severely physically handicapped   young to assume the
                                                responsibilities of parenthood

When pregnancy is the result of rape   ☐   When the mother-to-be is   ☐
                                                unmarried

When it is the only way to save the   ☐   On demand and available to   ☐
mother's life   all on the National Health

Other *(please specify)* _____

---

28. (a) Do you approve or disapprove of married couples using artificial methods of contraception? *(Please tick **one** box)*

        Approve ☐   Disapprove ☐

(b) If you **approve**, who should take the main responsibility? *(Please tick **one** box)*

    The Husband ☐   The Wife ☐   Both ☐

PART III

Now we come to Part III which is a short section about your neighbourhood.

1. Were you brought up in a Protestant, Catholic or mixed area of Northern Ireland? *(Please tick **one** box)*

Protestant	Mixed	Catholic	Not brought up in Northern Ireland
☐	☐	☐	☐

2. In what street / road do you live? (NOTE: *We do NOT want your address. We only need to know your neighbourhood*) If you live on a long road, please also give the name of a nearby side street; for example, Newtownards Road near Templemore Avenue.

_____

3. (a) How would you describe your neighbourhood now? *(Please tick one box)*

    All Protestant ☐
    Mostly Protestant ☐
    About equal numbers of Protestants and Catholics ☐
    Mostly Catholic ☐
    All Catholic ☐

    (b) What has happened to your neighbourhood over the last five years? *(please tick one box)*

    It has become much more Protestant ☐
    It has become a little more Protestant ☐
    It has stayed about the same ☐
    It has become a little more Catholic ☐
    It has become much more Catholic ☐

4. What kind of neighbourhood would you **prefer** to live in now? *(Please tick one box)*

    All Protestant ☐
    Mostly Protestant ☐
    About equal number Protestants and Catholics ☐
    Mostly Catholic ☐
    All Catholic ☐

5. People in Belfast have suffered during the present "Troubles".

    (a) Have you ever had to move house because of intimidation? *(Please tick)*

    YES ☐   NO ☐

(b) Has your home ever been bomb damaged? *(please tick)*

        YES ☐   NO ☐

(c) Have you ever had a relative, close friend or neighbour killed or seriously injured due to the "Troubles"? *(Please tick **one** box for each)*

	Yes	No		Yes	No		Yes	No
A Relative	☐	☐	A Close Friend	☐	☐	A Neighbour	☐	☐

PART IV

We now come to the final part of the survey. Here we would like to find out how you feel about certain aspects of life and society in Northern Ireland.

1. Who do you have more in common with? *(Please tick **one** box)*

    A Catholic of your own class   ☐
    or
    A Protestant of a different class   ☐

    Don't Know   ☐

2. (a) Which of the following schools would you **prefer** to send a child of yours to? *(Please tick **one** box)*

    A school in which all the pupils are Protestant   ☐

    A school in which most of the pupils are Protestant   ☐

    A school with more or less equal numbers of Protestant and Catholic pupils   ☐

    A school in which most of the pupils are Catholic   ☐

    (b) Whatever the mixture of pupils in the school, which school would you **prefer** to send a child of yours to? *(Please tick **one** box)*

    One with both Protestant and Catholic religious values   ☐

    One with Catholic religious values   ☐

    One with Protestant religious values   ☐

    Other *(please specify)* _____

3. Do you agree or disagree with this statement: "Catholic and Protestant school children should be encouraged to join together on school projects"? *(Please tick one box)*

Strongly Agree ☐   Agree ☐   Disagree ☐   Strongly Disagree ☐   Don't Know ☐

4. Would you be prepared to marry a non-Christian? *(Please tick one box)*

YES ☐   NO ☐

5. People are willing to have different relationships with different groups.

(a) Please read **each** of the following statements. For **each** group if your answer is YES please tick the box. **Tick as many boxes as you need.**

	Northern Irish Protestant	Northern Irish Catholic
I would be happy to marry	☐	☐
I would be happy to have as a nextdoor neighbour	☐	☐
I would be happy to work with	☐	☐
I would have no dealings at all with	☐	☐

(b) Please read **each** of the following statements. For **each** group if your answer is YES please tick the box. **Tick as many boxes as you need.**

	Indian	English	Chinese	Black	Southern Irish
I would be happy to marry	☐	☐	☐	☐	☐
I would be happy to have as a nextdoor neighbour	☐	☐	☐	☐	☐
I would be happy to work with	☐	☐	☐	☐	☐
I would have no dealings at all with	☐	☐	☐	☐	☐

6. Would you be happy to marry a person who is...? *(Please tick **as many** boxes as you require)*

	Yes		Yes		Yes
Pentecostal	☐	Baptist	☐	Jehovah's Witness	☐
Mormon	☐	Presbyterian	☐	Evangelical Presbyterian	☐
Church of Ireland	☐	Congregational	☐	Member of a Fellowship Church	☐
Free Presbyterian	☐	Methodist	☐	Reformed Presbyterian	☐
Quaker	☐	Brethren	☐	Non-Subscribing Presbyterian	☐

I would not be happy to marry any of these ☐

7. Do you agree or disagree with these statements:

(a) "To-day in Northern Ireland Catholics generally get a fair deal."
*(Please tick **one** box)*

Strongly Agree	Agree	Disagree	Strongly Disagree
☐	☐	☐	☐

(b) "To-day in Northern Ireland Protestants generally get a fair deal."
*(Please tick **one** box)*

Strongly Agree	Agree	Disagree	Strongly Disagree
☐	☐	☐	☐

8. (a) Do you think a person's religion matters in getting a good job in Northern Ireland these days? *(Please tick **one** box)*

YES ☐   NO ☐

(b) If YES, which matters most? *(Please tick **one** box)*

Being a Catholic ☐   Being a Protestant ☐

9. In which of the following circumstances would it be all right for a woman to go out to work? *(Please tick **many** boxes as you require)*

	Yes	No
A woman without children	☐	☐
A woman with children under school age	☐	☐
A woman with children of school age	☐	☐
A woman with grown-up children	☐	☐

None of these—"A woman's place is in the home" ☐

10. Within a marriage who should take charge of the money? *(Please tick **one** box)*

Husband ☐   Wife ☐   Both together ☐

11. Do you agree or disagree with the following: *(Please tick **one** box for each)*

	Strongly Agree	Agree	Disagree	Strongly Disagree	Don't Know
"Schools should bring back the cane"	☐	☐	☐	☐	☐
"Courts let wrongdoers off too lightly"	☐	☐	☐	☐	☐
"Capital punishment should be allowed in certain circumstances"	☐	☐	☐	☐	☐

12. Which of the following activities would you be prepared to take part in on a Sunday? *(Please tick **as many** boxes as you require)*

	Yes		Yes
Attending a sports event	☐	Watching T.V.	☐
Shopping	☐	Going to the cinema / theatre	☐
Buying a Sunday newspaper	☐	Using a recreation centre	☐
Having a meal in a restaurant	☐	None of these	☐

13. If you were given complete freedom of choice, which **one** country outside Northern Ireland would you choose to live in?

_____

14. Are you more likely to consider leaving Northern Ireland now than a few years ago? *(Please tick one box)*

    Yes ☐ If Yes, Why? _____
    No ☐

15. Which of these terms best describes how you usually think of yourself? *(Please tick one box)*

    An Ulsterman/woman ☐   Irish   ☐
    Northern Irish   ☐   Ulster British ☐
    British   ☐   British Irish ☐
    Ulster Irish   ☐

    Other *(please specify)* ☐ _____

16. How would you usually describe where you live? *(Please tick one box)*

    The North   ☐   The North of Ireland ☐
    The Six Counties ☐   Ulster   ☐
    Northern Ireland ☐   Ireland   ☐

    Other *(please specify)* ☐ _____

17. (a) At the moment which political party in Northern Ireland **comes closest** to expressing your own views?

    _____

    (b) Why do you favour this party?

    _____

18. (a) To what extent do you think people "across the water" understand why many Ulster Protestants want to maintain the Union with Great Britain? *(Please tick one box)*

    Not at all ☐   A little ☐   A lot ☐   Completely ☐

    (b) To what extent do you think people "across the water" understand why many Catholics in Northern Ireland want a United Ireland? *(Please tick one box)*

    Not at all ☐   A little ☐   A lot ☐   Completely ☐

19. Which ONE of the following reasons do you think best explains why many Protestants in Northern Ireland object to a United Ireland? *(Please tick one box)*

    Because they would be a minority in it ☐

    Because they would want to keep their privileged position in Northern Ireland ☐

    Because they fear their standard of living would go down ☐

    Because they are afraid of losing their British identity ☐

    Because they fear the power the Roman Catholic Church would have in a United Ireland ☐

    Other *(please specify)* _____

20. Which ONE of the following reasons do you think best explains why many Catholics in Northern Ireland want a United Ireland? *(Please tick one box)*

    Because they would be a majority in it ☐
    Because they would gain a privileged position in a United Ireland ☐
    Because they hope their standard of living would go up ☐
    Because they could express their Irish identity ☐
    Because they would prefer to live in a Catholic country ☐

    Other *(please specify)* _____

21. (a) Some people say that at a time in the future more than half the population of Northern Ireland will be Catholic. Do you agree or disagree? *(Please tick)*

    Agree ☐   Disagree ☐

    (b) If you answered **AGREE**, when do you think Catholics will become the majority in Northern Ireland? *(please tick one box)*

    Within the next 5 years   ☐   Within the next 40 years   ☐
    Within the next 10 years ☐   Within the next 50 years   ☐
    Within the next 20 years ☐   Within the next 100 years   ☐
    Within the next 30 years ☐   More than 100 years from now ☐

22. How do you react to this statement: "The Gospel can only flourish in Northern Ireland if it remains separate from the Republic of Ireland." *(Please tick one box)*

    Strongly Agree   Agree   Disagree   Strongly Disagree   Don't Know
        ☐   ☐   ☐   ☐   ☐

23. Which of these terms do you think best describes how people "across the water" think of Protestants in Northern Ireland? *(Please tick one box)*

    Ulstermen/women   ☐   Irish   ☐
    Northern Irish   ☐   Ulster British ☐
    British   ☐   British Irish   ☐
    Ulster Irish   ☐

    Other *(please specify)*   ☐   _____

24. How do you react to these statements? *(Please tick one box for each)*

	Strongly Agree	Agree	Disagree	Strongly Disagree
"The Catholic community is strongly united"	☐	☐	☐	☐
"The Protestant community is strongly united"	☐	☐	☐	☐

25. Are the "Troubles" in Northern Ireland today **mainly** about politics or **mainly** about religion? *(Please tick one box)*

    Politics ☐   Religion ☐

26. Do you approve or disapprove of the Orange Order? *(Please tick **one** box)*

Strongly Approve	Approve	Disapprove	Strongly Disapprove	Don't Know
☐	☐	☐	☐	☐

27. Do you agree or disagree with this statement: " Dealing with the security situation in Northern Ireland should be left **entirely** to the security forces." *(Please tick **one** box)*

Strongly Agree	Agree	Disagree	Strongly Disagree
☐	☐	☐	☐

28. What do you think the long term political future of Northern Ireland should be? *(Please tick **one** box)*

Northern Ireland should remain part of the United Kingdom ☐
Northern Ireland should become united with the rest of Ireland ☐
Northern Ireland should become independent ☐

Other *(please specify)* _____

Thank You very much indeed for all your help. We really appreciate the time and effort you have spent in completing this survey.

Please put your completed questionnaire in the envelope, seal and return to the box provided.

Thank You.

Would you be interested in helping us further? If so please phone Jahnet at Queen's University, on Belfast 335087

If you have any comments about the questionnaire, or the issues it deals with, we would be very interested to have them. Please use the space provided overleaf.

Comments

Appendix III

Catholic Questionnaire

SURVEY OF BELFAST CHURCHGOERS 1993

Over the past number of years we have all seen changes, religious, social and political, in Northern Ireland. At present we are carrying out a study of how churchgoers feel about these changes. This study will be carried out among churchgoers of all denominations.

Your church is in one of the areas that has been chosen to be part of the survey. A number of people from each church are being asked to help by answering our questionnaire, and we very much hope that you will be able to find time to take part. Most of the questions only require you to tick a box.

We can assure you that every answer will be treated in the strictest confidence. We don't know who you are; we only want to know your parish and what area you live in.

The results of this survey will be extremely valuable for understanding people's responses to many of the major changes that have been taking place in our society.

After filling in the questionnaire, please place it in the envelope provided, seal it, and place it in the collection box in the church porch.

Thank you.

Belfast Churchgoers Survey 1993
St. Mary's College of Education
191 Falls Road
Belfast, BT12 6FE

PART 1

In this first part of the survey we want to ask you some general questions about yourself and your family.

1. Are you male or female? *(Please tick)* Male ☐ Female ☐

---

2. Are you....? *(Please tick one box)*

   Single ☐   Married ☐   Separated ☐   Divorced ☐   Widowed ☐   Other ☐

---

3. (a) Do you have children? *(Please tick)* YES ☐   NO ☐

   (b) If YES, how many? *(Please tick one box)*

   1 ☐   2 ☐   3 ☐   4 ☐   5+ ☐

---

4. What age are you? *(Please tick one box)*

   17 and under ☐   18-24 ☐   25-34 ☐   35-44 ☐   45-54 ☐   55-64 ☐   65 and over ☐

---

5. Is your home....? *(Please tick one box)*

   Rented from the Housing Executive ☐
   Owner Occupied ☐
   Other ☐

---

6. What type of school / college did you last attend full time? *(Please tick one box)*

   Primary/Elementary ☐   F.E. College/Technical College ☐
   Secondary/Intermediate ☐   University/Poly/College of Education ☐
   Grammar ☐   Other *(please specify)* ☐
   _____

7. (a) What was the home background in which **you were brought up**? *(Please tick one box)*

    | Professional | ☐ | Semi-Skilled Manual | ☐ |
    | Managerial | ☐ | Unskilled Manual | ☐ |
    | Skilled Manual | ☐ | Other *(please specify)* | ☐ |
    | Clerical / Sales| ☐ | _____ | |

    (b) What is your **present** home background? *(Please tick one box)*

    | Professional | ☐ | Semi-Skilled Manual | ☐ |
    | Managerial | ☐ | Unskilled Manual | ☐ |
    | Skilled Manual | ☐ | Other *(please specify)* | ☐ |
    | Clerical / Sales| ☐ | _____ | |

8. (a) Have you ever been employed? *(Please tick)*   **YES** ☐   **NO** ☐

    (b) If **YES**, please tell us what your occupation is (or was). Please describe the job as precisely as possible.

    _____

    (c) At present, are you....? *(please tick one box)*

    | Employed: Full time | ☐ | Student/Pupil | ☐ |
    | Employed: Part time | ☐ | Permanently sick/Disabled | ☐ |
    | Unemployed : Short term (1 yr or less) | ☐ | Y.T.P. | ☐ |
    | Unemployed : Long term (1 yr+) | ☐ | Retired | ☐ |
    | Looking after home / family | ☐ | Other | ☐ |

9. (a) Are you the head of your household? *(Please tick)*   **YES** ☐   **NO** ☐

    (b) If **NO**, please describe what your head of household's occupation is (or was).

    _____

    Never had a job ☐

PART II

We would now like to ask you some questions about your religious views.

1. (a) Have you always been a Catholic? *(Please tick)*

    YES ☐   NO ☐

   (b) If your answer is NO, please tell us the name of your previous religion / denomination, if any?

   _____

2. (a) Which parish do you belong to?

   _____

   (b) Which church do you go to most frequently?

   _____

3. How do you normally get to church? *(please tick **one** box)*

Walk	Church Bus	Public Transport	Car	Other
☐	☐	☐	☐	☐

4. (a) Have you ever held either of the following lay positions in the church? *(Please tick)*

    Eucharistic Minister ☐   Reader ☐

   (b) Have you ever held a position of leadership in any parish group? *(Please tick)*

    YES ☐   NO ☐

5. About how often do you go to ...? *(Please tick one box for **each** column)*

	Mass	Communion	Confession
Daily	☐	☐	☐
Twice a week or more	☐	☐	☐
Once a week	☐	☐	☐
2-3 times a month	☐	☐	☐
Once a month	☐	☐	☐
Several times a year	☐	☐	☐
Once a year	☐	☐	☐
Less than once a year	☐	☐	☐
Never	☐	☐	☐

6. About how often do you pray in private? *(Please tick **one** box)*

Twice a day or more ☐   Sometimes but not regularly ☐
Once a day ☐   Rarely / Only on special occasions ☐
Several times a week ☐   Never ☐
Once a week ☐

7. Do you read the Scriptures apart from in church? *(Please tick **one** box)*

Once a day or more ☐   Sometimes but not regularly ☐
Several times a week ☐   Rarely or only on special occasions ☐
Once a week ☐   Never ☐

8. Do you ever....? *(Please tick as many boxes as you require)*

	Yes		Yes
Say the Rosary	☐	Wear religious medals	☐
Pray to certain Saints	☐	Wear scapulars	☐
Do the Stations of the Cross	☐	Do penance on Friday	☐
Say family prayers	☐	Use Holy Water at home	☐

9. Could you tell us how firmly you believe in the following?
   (Please tick one box for each)

	Believe Firmly	Believe With Difficulty	Partly Believe/ Partly Reject	Unsure	Reject
The Resurrection of Christ	☐	☐	☐	☐	☐
The Bible is the Word of God	☐	☐	☐	☐	☐
People can sin	☐	☐	☐	☐	☐
There is life after death	☐	☐	☐	☐	☐
There is a Heaven	☐	☐	☐	☐	☐
The Devil exists	☐	☐	☐	☐	☐
There is a Hell	☐	☐	☐	☐	☐

10. Could you tell us how firmly you believe in the following?
    (Please tick one box for each)

	Believe Firmly	Believe With Difficulty	Partly Believe/ Partly Reject	Unsure	Reject
Miracles of healing happen today	☐	☐	☐	☐	☐
Some people today have the gift of 'speaking in tongues'	☐	☐	☐	☐	☐

11. Could you tell us how firmly you believe in the following?
    (Please tick one box for each)

	Believe Firmly	Believe With Difficulty	Partly Believe/ Partly Reject	Unsure	Reject
The Assumption of Our Lady	☐	☐	☐	☐	☐
The Immaculate Conception	☐	☐	☐	☐	☐
Papal Infallibility	☐	☐	☐	☐	☐
Sins are forgiven in Confession	☐	☐	☐	☐	☐
That the bread & wine are changed into the Body and Blood of Christ at Mass	☐	☐	☐	☐	☐
The Catholic Church is the one true church	☐	☐	☐	☐	☐

12. Would you say that you have had a turning point in your life when you committed yourself to Christ? *(Please tick)*

    YES ☐   NO ☐   Don't Know ☐

13. Which one of the following do you think is the most important guide to living a Christian life? *(Please tick one box)*

    The Scriptures ☐
    Scriptures and Church Teachings ☐
    The Individual's Conscience ☐

14. Do you agree or disagree with this statement: "Every passage in the Bible should be taken literally"? *(Please tick one box)*

Strongly Agree ☐   Agree ☐   Disagree ☐   Strongly Disagree ☐   Don't Know ☐

15. Do you agree or disagree with this statement: " People were better off in the old days when they knew just how they were expected to act"? *(Please tick one box)*

Strongly Agree ☐   Agree ☐   Disagree ☐   Strongly Disagree ☐   Don't Know ☐

16. Which would you prefer to hear read from Scriptures in church? *(Please tick one box)*

    "Let us make **man** in our image" ☐
    or
    "Let us make **humankind** in our image" ☐

17. Do you agree with lay people distributing Holy Communion :

    (a) at Mass?   YES ☐   NO ☐   *(Please tick one box)*

    (b) to the Sick?   YES ☐   NO ☐   *(Please tick one box)*

18. (a) Do you think women are given enough responsibility in the Catholic Church? *(Please tick one box)*

    YES ☐   NO ☐   Don't Know ☐

(b) Do you agree with women having the following roles? *(Please tick **one** box for each)*

	Strongly Agree	Agree	Unsure	Disagree	Strongly Disagree
Eucharistic Ministers	☐	☐	☐	☐	☐
Altar Servers	☐	☐	☐	☐	☐

(c) Would you agree with women priests in the Catholic Church? *(Please tick **one** box)*

Strongly Agree	Agree	Unsure	Disagree	Strongly Disagree
☐	☐	☐	☐	☐

---

19. How important is membership of the Catholic Church to you? *(Please tick **one** box)*

All Important	Extremely Important	Very Important	Important	Not Very Important	Not At All Important
☐	☐	☐	☐	☐	☐

---

20. Which Protestant Church do you think is **closest in doctrine** to Catholicism?

    _____

---

21. (a) Have you ever attended an Ecumenical Service of Catholics and Protestants? *(Please tick)*

    YES ☐   NO ☐

(b) With which of the following would you be happy to take part in a joint service of worship? *(Please tick **as many** boxes as you require)*

Church of Ireland	☐	Methodist	☐
Presbyterian	☐	Quaker	☐
Congregational	☐	Pentecostal	☐
Reformed Presbyterian	☐	Non-Subscribing Presbyterian	☐
Free Presbyterian	☐	Salvation Army	☐
Baptist	☐	Evangelical Presbyterian	☐
Brethren	☐		

None Of These ☐

22. Which of the following statements comes closest to what you feel about future relations between the Protestant and Catholic churches? *(Please tick one box)*

    They should aim for unity □

    They should not aim for unity but for
      greater co-operation in religious and social matters □

    They should not aim for unity but for
      greater co-operation in social matters only □

    They should not aim for unity nor for greater
      co-operation on anything □

23. How active do you think the churches should be in trying to improve relations between the communities in Northern Ireland? *(Please tick one box)*

    Much more active than now □   A little less active than now □
    A little more active than now □   Much less active than now □
    About the same as now □   Don't Know □

24. Are you, or have you been, actively involved in cross-community organizations? *(Please tick one box)*

    YES □   NO □

    If YES, which? _____

25. (a) Do you agree or disagree with these statements: "Sermons should deal with Northern Ireland's social and economic problems on at least some occasions." *(Please tick one box)*

    Strongly Agree   Agree   Disagree   Strongly Disagree   Don't Know
        □   □   □   □   □

    (b) "Sermons should deal with Northern Ireland's political problems on at least some occasions." *(Please tick one box)*

    Strongly Agree   Agree   Disagree   Strongly Disagree   Don't Know
        □   □   □   □   □

26. What do you think about the following **moral** issues: *(Please tick one box for each)*

	Always Wrong	Generally Wrong	Depends	Generally Right	Always Right
Sex before marriage	☐	☐	☐	☐	☐
Living together outside marriage	☐	☐	☐	☐	☐
Abortion	☐	☐	☐	☐	☐
Homosexual Practice	☐	☐	☐	☐	☐

27. Are there ever any circumstances in which you think civil divorce is acceptable? *(Please tick as many boxes as you require)*

Under no circumstances	☐	When desertion occurs	☐
When adultery is committed	☐	When the partners are not suited	☐
When physical violence occurs	☐	When the marriage breaks down	☐
When mental cruelty occurs	☐		

Other *(please specify)* _____

28. Are there ever any circumstances in which abortion should be **legally** available? *(Please tick as many boxes as you require)*

When the couple do not want another child	☐	No, not in any circumstances	☐
When it is likely that the child will be born severely physically handicapped	☐	When the mother-to-be is too young to assume the responsibilities of parenthood	☐
When pregnancy is the result of rape	☐	When the mother-to-be is unmarried	☐
When it is the only way to save the mother's life	☐	On demand and available to all on the National Health	☐

Other *(please specify)* _____

29. What would you think of the following actions for a Catholic? *(Please tick **one** box for each)*

	Always Wrong	Generally Wrong	Depends	Generally Right	Always Right
Missing Mass on Sunday	☐	☐	☐	☐	☐
Not bringing children up as Catholics	☐	☐	☐	☐	☐
Not sending children to a Catholic School	☐	☐	☐	☐	☐
Married couples using artifical methods of contraception	☐	☐	☐	☐	☐

PART III

Now we come to Part III which is a short section about your neighbourhood.

1. Were you brought up in a Catholic, Protestant or mixed area of Northern Ireland? *(Please tick one box)*

Catholic	Mixed	Protestant	Not brought up in Northern Ireland
☐	☐	☐	☐

2. In what street / road do you live? (NOTE: *We do **NOT** want your address. We only need to know your neighbourhood*) If you live on a long road, please also give the name of a nearby side street; for example, Falls Road near Broadway.

   _____

3. (a) How would you describe your neighbourhood now? *(Please tick **one** box)*

All Catholic	☐
Mostly Catholic	☐
About equal numbers of Catholics and Protestants	☐
Mostly Protestant	☐
All Protestant	☐

(b) What has happened to your neighbourhood over the last five years? *(Please tick one box)*

It has become much more Catholic ☐
It has become a little more Catholic ☐
It has stayed about the same ☐
It has become a little more Protestant ☐
It has become much more Protestant ☐

4. What kind of neighbourhood would you **prefer** to live in now? *(Please tick one box)*

All Catholic ☐
Mostly Catholic ☐
About equal number Catholics and Protestants ☐
Mostly Protestant ☐
All Protestant ☐

5. People in Belfast have suffered during the present "Troubles".

(a) Have you ever had to move house because of intimidation? *(Please tick)*

YES ☐   NO ☐

(b) Has your home ever been bomb damaged? *(Please tick)*

YES ☐   NO ☐

(c) Have you ever had a relative, close friend or neighbour killed or seriously injured due to the "Troubles"? *(Please tick one box for each)*

	Yes	No		Yes	No		Yes	No
A Relative	☐	☐	A Close Friend	☐	☐	A Neighbour	☐	☐

PART IV

We now come to the final part of the survey. Here we would like to find out how you feel about certain aspects of life and society in Northern Ireland.

1. Who do you have more in common with? (*Please tick **one** box*)

    A Protestant of your own class ☐
    or
    A Catholic of a different class ☐

    Don't Know ☐

2. (a) Which of the following schools would you **prefer** to send a child of yours to? (*Please tick **one** box*)

    A school in which all the pupils are Catholic ☐

    A school in which most of the pupils are Catholic ☐

    A school with more or less equal numbers of Protestant and Catholic pupils ☐

    A school in which most of the pupils are Protestant ☐

    (b) Whatever the mixture of pupils in the school, which school would you **prefer** to send a child of yours to? (*Please tick **one** box*)

    One with both Catholic and Protestant religious values ☐

    One with Catholic religious values ☐

    One with Protestant religious values ☐

    Other (*please specify*) _____

3. Do you agree or disagree with this statement: "Catholic and Protestant school children should be encouraged to join together on school projects"? (*Please tick **one** box*)

    Strongly Agree   Agree   Disagree   Strongly Disagree   Don't Know
    ☐   ☐   ☐   ☐   ☐

4. How important is it for you to marry a Catholic? *(Please tick one box)*

Extremely Important	Very Important	Important	Not Very Important	Not At All Important
☐	☐	☐	☐	☐

5. People are willing to have different relationships with different groups.

(a) Please read **each** of the following statements. For **each** group if your answer is YES please tick the box. **Tick as many boxes as you need.**

	Northern Irish Catholic	Northern Irish Protestant
I would be happy to marry	☐	☐
I would be happy to have as a nextdoor neighbour	☐	☐
I would be happy to work with	☐	☐
I would have no dealings at all with	☐	☐

(b) Please read **each** of the following statements. For **each** group if your answer is YES please tick the box. **Tick as many boxes as you need.**

	Indian	English	Chinese	Black	Southern Irish
I would be happy to marry	☐	☐	☐	☐	☐
I would be happy to have as a nextdoor neighbour	☐	☐	☐	☐	☐
I would be happy to work with	☐	☐	☐	☐	☐
I would have no dealings at all with	☐	☐	☐	☐	☐

6. Would you be happy to marry a person who is...? *(Please tick as many boxes as you require)*

	Yes		Yes		Yes
Presbyterian	☐	Free Presbyterian	☐	Methodist	☐
Pentecostal	☐	Church of Ireland	☐	Brethren	☐
Mormon	☐	Jehovah's Witness	☐	Baptist	☐

I would not be happy to marry any of these ☐

7. Do you agree or disagree with these statements:

    (a) "To-day in Northern Ireland Catholics generally get a fair deal." *(Please tick one box)*

    Strongly Agree ☐   Agree ☐   Disagree ☐   Strongly Disagree ☐

    (b) "To-day in Northern Ireland Protestants generally get a fair deal." *(Please tick one box)*

    Strongly Agree ☐   Agree ☐   Disagree ☐   Strongly Disagree ☐

8. (a) Do you think a person's religion matters in getting a good job in Northern Ireland these days? *(Please tick one box)*

    YES ☐   NO ☐

    (b) If **YES**, which matters most? *(Please tick one box)*

    Being a Catholic ☐   Being a Protestant ☐

9. In which of the following circumstances would it be all right for a woman to go out to work? *(Please tick as many boxes as you require)*

	Yes	No
A woman without children	☐	☐
A woman with children under school age	☐	☐
A woman with children of school age	☐	☐
A woman with grown-up children	☐	☐

None of these—"A woman's place is in the home" ☐

10. Within a marriage who should take charge of the money? *(Please tick **one** box)*

    Husband ☐   Wife ☐   Both together ☐

11. Do you agree or disagree with the following: *(Please tick one box for each)*

	Strongly Agree	Agree	Disagree	Strongly Disagree	Don't Know
"Schools should bring back the cane"	☐	☐	☐	☐	☐
"Courts let wrongdoers off too lightly"	☐	☐	☐	☐	☐
"Capital punishment should be allowed in certain circumstances"	☐	☐	☐	☐	☐

12. Which of the following activities would you be prepared to take part in on a Sunday? *(Please tick **as many** boxes as you require)*

	Yes		Yes
Attending a sports event	☐	Watching T.V.	☐
Shopping	☐	Going to the cinema / theatre	☐
Buying a Sunday newspaper	☐	Using a recreation centre	☐
Having a meal in a restaurant	☐	None of these	☐

13. If you were given complete freedom of choice, which **one** country outside Northern Ireland would you choose to live in?

    _____

14. Are you more likely to consider leaving Northern Ireland now than a few years ago? *(Please tick **one** box)*

    Yes ☐   If **Yes**, Why? _____
    No ☐

15. Which of these terms best describes how you usually think of yourself? *(Please tick one box)*

    An Ulsterman/woman ☐   Irish ☐
    Northern Irish ☐   Ulster British ☐
    British ☐   British Irish ☐
    Ulster Irish ☐

    Other *(please specify)* ☐ _____

16. How would you usually describe where you live? *(Please tick one box)*

    The North ☐   The North of Ireland ☐
    The Six Counties ☐   Ulster ☐
    Northern Ireland ☐   Ireland ☐

    Other *(please specify)* ☐ _____

17. (a) At the moment which political party in Northern Ireland **comes closest** to expressing your own views?

    _____

    (b) Why do you favour this party?

    _____

18. (a) To what extent do you think people "across the water" understand why many Ulster Protestants want to maintain the Union with Great Britain? *(Please tick one box)*

    Not at all   A little   A lot   Completely
       ☐   ☐   ☐   ☐

    (b) To what extent do you think people "across the water" understand why many Catholics in Northern Ireland want a United Ireland? *(Please tick one box)*

    Not at all   A little   A lot   Completely
       ☐   ☐   ☐   ☐

19. Which **ONE** of the following reasons do you think best explains why many Protestants in Northern Ireland object to a United Ireland? *(Please tick one box)*

    Because they would be a minority in it ☐

    Because they would want to keep their privileged position in Northern Ireland ☐

    Because they fear their standard of living would go down ☐

    Because they are afraid of losing their British identity ☐

    Because they fear the power the Roman Catholic Church would have in a United Ireland ☐

    Other *(please specify)* _____

20. Which **ONE** of the following reasons do you think best explains why many Catholics in Northern Ireland want a United Ireland? *(Please tick one box)*

    Because they would be a majority in it ☐
    Because they would gain a privileged position in a United Ireland ☐
    Because they hope their standard of living would go up ☐
    Because they could express their Irish identity ☐
    Because they would prefer to live in a Catholic country ☐

    Other *(please specify)* _____

21. (a) Some people say that at a time in the future more than half the population of Northern Ireland will be Catholic. Do you agree or disagree? *(Please tick)*

    Agree ☐   Disagree ☐

(b) If you answered **AGREE**, when do you think Catholics will become the majority in Northern Ireland? *(Please tick **one** box)*

Within the next 5 years ☐ Within the next 40 years ☐
Within the next 10 years ☐ Within the next 50 years ☐
Within the next 20 years ☐ Within the next 100 years ☐
Within the next 30 years ☐ More than 100 years from now ☐

22. How do you react to this statement: "The Catholic faith can only flourish here if Ireland is united." *(Please tick **one** box)*

Strongly Agree   Agree   Disagree   Strongly Disagree   Don't Know
       ☐   ☐   ☐   ☐   ☐

23. Which of these terms do you think best describes how people "across the water" think of Catholics in Northern Ireland? *(Please tick **one** box)*

Ulstermen/women ☐ Irish ☐
Northern Irish ☐ Ulster British ☐
British ☐ British Irish ☐
Ulster Irish ☐

Other *(please specify)* ☐ _____

24. How do you react to these statements? *(Please tick **one** box for each)*

	Strongly Agree	Agree	Disagree	Strongly Disagree
"The Catholic community is strongly united"	☐	☐	☐	☐
"The Protestant community is strongly united"	☐	☐	☐	☐

25. Are the "Troubles" in Northern Ireland today **mainly** about politics or **mainly** about religion? *(Please tick **one** box)*

Politics ☐   Religion ☐

26. Do you agree or disagree with this statement: "Dealing with the security situation in Northern Ireland should be left **entirely** to the security forces." *(Please tick **one** box)*

Strongly Agree   Agree   Disagree   Strongly Disagree
      ☐   ☐   ☐   ☐

27. What do you think the long term political future of Northern Ireland should be? *(Please tick **one** box)*

Northern Ireland should remain part of the United Kingdom   ☐
Northern Ireland should become united with the rest of Ireland   ☐
Northern Ireland should become independent   ☐

Other *(please specify)* _____

Thank You very much indeed for all your help. We really appreciate the time and effort you have spent in completing this survey.

Please put your completed questionnaire in the envelope, seal and return to the box provided.

Thank You.

**Would you be interested in helping us further?
If so please phone Rebecca at St. Mary's College of Education, Falls Road, on Belfast 238408**

If you have any comments about the questionnaire we would be very interested to have them. Please use the space provided overleaf.

Comments

Appendix IV

Private and Public Morality Scales

Private Morality Scale

Attitudes to four issues provided the basis of the private morality scale. These were: sex before marriage, living together outside marriage, abortion, and homosexual practice. Points were allocated as follows:

> Always wrong   = 1
> Generally wrong = 2
> Depends   = 3
> Generally right = 4
> Always right   = 5

When points were accumulated, each respondent was categorised using the following scale:

> 4   = Strict
> 5-6   = Strict / Moderate
> 7-9   = Moderate / Liberal
> 10-20 = Liberal

Public Morality Scale

Attitudes to three issues provided the basis of the public morality scale. These were: caning in schools, court leniency, and capital punishment in certain circumstances. Points were allocated as follows:

> Strongly agree   = 1
> Agree   = 2
> Disagree   = 3
> Strongly disgree = 4

When points were accumulated, each respondent was categorised using the following scale:

> 3   = Strict
> 4-6   = Strict / Moderate
> 7-9   = Moderate / Liberal
> 10-12 = Liberal

Bibliography

Akenson, D.H. (1991), *Small Difference: Irish Catholics and Irish Protestants 1815-1922. International Perspectives,* Gill and Macmillan, Dublin.

Boal, F.W. and Livingstone, D.N. (1986), Protestants in Belfast: A View from the Inside, *Contemporary Review,* Vol. 248, 169-175.

Boal, F.W., Campbell, J.A. and Livingstone, D.N. (1985), Protestants and Social Change in the Belfast Area: A Socio-Geographical Study. Research Report to the Economic and Social Research Council, Ref. No. G0023/0025.

Boal, F.W., Campbell, J.A. and Livingstone, D.N. (1991), The Protestant Mosaic: A Majority of Minorities, in P.J. Roche and B. Barton (eds), *The Northern Ireland Question: Myth and Reality,* Avebury, Aldershot.

Bogardus, E. (1925), Measuring Social Distances, *Journal of Applied Sociology,* Vol. 9, pp. 216-226.

Breslin, A. and Weafer, J. (1984), *Religious Beliefs, Practice and Moral Attitudes: A Comparison of Two Irish Surveys 1974-1984,* Council for Research and Development, Maynooth.

Dunlop, J. (1995), *A Precarious Belonging,* Blackstaff Press, Belfast.

Eames, R . (1992), *Chains To Be Broken: A Personal Reflection on Northern Ireland and Its People,* Weidenfield and Nicolson, London.

Fogarty, M., Ryan, L. and Lee, J. (1984), *Irish Values and Attitudes,* Dominican Publications, Dublin.

Galliher, J.F., and DeGregory, J.L. (1985), *Violence in Northern Ireland: Understanding Protestant Perspectives,* Gill and Macmillan, Dublin.

Jenkins, R., Donnan, H. and McFarlane, G. (1986), *The Sectarian Divide in Northern Ireland Today*, Royal Anthropological Institute, London.

Keane, M.C, (1990), Segregation Processes in Public Sector Housing, in Doherty, P. (ed.) *Geographical Perspectives on the Belfast Region*, Geographical Society of Ireland Special Publications, Newtownabbey.

Kirby, P. (1984), *Is Irish Catholicism Dying?* Mercier Press, Cork.

Kung, H. (1986), *Church and Change; The Irish Experience*, Gill and Macmillan, Dublin.

Inglis, T. (1987), *Moral Monopoly: The Catholic Church in Modern Irish Society*, Gill and Macmillan, Dublin.

Ley, D. (1973), *The Black Inner City as Frontier Outpost. Images and Behaviour of a Philadelphia Neighborhood*, Association of American Geographers, Washington, D.C.

Loughran, G. (1987), The Rationale of Catholic Education, in R.D. Osborne, R.J. Cormack and R.L. Miller (eds) *Education and Policy in Northern Ireland*, Policy Research Institute, The Queen's University of Belfast and The University of Ulster, Belfast and Jordanstown.

Lyons, F.S.L. (1979a), *The Burden of Our History. The W.B. Rankin Memorial Lecture delivered before The Queen's University of Belfast on 4th December 1978*, The Queen's University of Belfast, Belfast.

Lyons, F.S.L. (1979b), *Culture and Anarchy in Ireland, 1890-1939*, Clarendon Press, Oxford.

McBrien, R.P. (1980), *Catholicism*, Geoffrey Chapman, London.

McDonagh, E. (1986), *Irish Challenges to Theology*, Dominican Publications, Dublin.

McElroy, G. (1991), *The Catholic Church and the Northern Ireland Crisis 1968-86*, Gill and Macmillan, Dublin.

McEwan, A. and Robinson, E. (1994), Evangelical Beliefs, Attitudes Towards Schooling and Educational Outcomes, *Research in Education*, Vol. 52, 65-74.

MacGréil, M. (1977), *Prejudice and Tolerance in Ireland*, College of Industrial Relations, Dublin.
MacGréil, M. (1991), *Religious Practice and Attitudes in Ireland*, Survey and Research Unit, Dept of Social Studies, St Patrick's College, Maynooth.
MacIntyre, A. (1985), *After Virtue: A Study in Moral Theory*, 2nd ed., Duckworth, London.
McMackin, T. (1993), Religious Faith and Integrated Schools, in C. Moffat (ed.) *Education Together for a Change: Integrated Education and Community Relations*, Fortnight Educational Trust, Belfast.
MacMahon, B. (1982), *A Study of Religion Among Dublin Adolescents*, Council for Research and Development, Maynooth.
Martin, D. (1982), Revived Dogma and New Cult, *Daedalus*, Vol. 111.
Moffat, C. (ed.) (1993), *Education Together for a Change: Integrated Education and Community Relations*, Fortnight Educational Trust, Belfast.
Morrow, D (1991), *The Churches and Inter-Community Relationships*, Centre for the Study of Conflict, The University of Ulster, Coleraine.
Murray, D. (1985), *Worlds Apart: Segregated Schools in Northern Ireland*, Appletree Press, Belfast.
Murray, D. (1990), *Secularism and The New Europe*, Veritas Publications, Dublin.
Nic Giolla Phádraig, M. (1974), *A Survey of Religious Practice: Attitudes amd Beliefs in the Republic of Ireland*, Research and Development Unit of the Catholic Communications Institute of Ireland, Dublin.
Northern Ireland Registrar General (1992), *Northern Ireland Census 1991: Belfast Urban Area Report*, HMSO, Belfast.
O'Brien, C.C. (1972), *States of Ireland*, Hutchinson, London.
O'Connor, F. (1993), *In Search of a State: Catholics in Northern Ireland*, Blackstaff Press, Belfast.

O'Doherty, P. (1994), *Church as Sacrament,* Columba Press, Dublin.

Osborne, R.D., R.J. Cormack, R.J. and Miller, R.L., (eds), (1987), *Education and Policy in Northern Ireland,* Policy Research Institute, The Queen's University of Belfast and The University of Ulster, Belfast and Jordanstown.

O'Sullivan, O. (1994), The Silent Schism, *The Furrow,* Vol. 45, 3-10.

Research and Development Commission (1978), *Students and Religion 1976,* Council for Research and Development, Maynooth.

Rose, R. (1971), *Governing Without Consensus:An Irish Perspective,* Faber and Faber Ltd, London.

Rose, R. (1976), *Northern Ireland: A Time of Choice,* Macmillan, London.

Said, E.W. (1978), *Orientalism,* Routledge and Kegan Paul, London.

Stringer, P. and Robinson, G. (eds) (1991), *Social Attitudes in Northern Ireland: The First Report,* Blackstaff Press, Belfast.

Stringer, P. and Robinson, G. (eds) (1992), *Social Attitudes in Northern Ireland: The Second Report,* Blackstaff Press, Belfast.

Stringer, P. and Robinson, G. (eds) (1993), *Social Attitudes in Northern Ireland: The Third Report,* Blackstaff Press, Belfast.

Todd, J. (1987), Two Traditions in Unionist Political Culture, *Irish Political Studies,* Vol. 2, 1-26.

Wallis, R., Bruce, S., and Taylor, D. (1986), *"No Surrender": Paisleyism in Northern Ireland,* The Queen's University of Belfast, Belfast.

Whelan, C. (ed.) (1994), *Values and Social Change in Ireland,* Gill and Macmillan, Dublin.

Whyte, J. (1990), *Interpreting Northern Ireland,* Clarendon Press, Oxford.

Index

abortion: Catholic attitudes to 37-38; Protestant attitudes to 70-71, 107-108, 109; comparison of Catholic and Protestant attitudes 151-152

age: and Catholic churchgoers 7; influence on attendance at Mass 12-14; influence on attendance at confession 12-14; and Catholic beliefs 21-22; and Catholic orthodoxy 25; and importance of religion to Catholics 29-30; and attitudes to discipline in society 40; and religious mixing 44; and attitudes to mixed marriage 51-52; and Protestant churchgoers 68; and beliefs about conversion 69; and biblical inerrancy 69; and sexual morality 70; and Protestant attitudes to abortion 71; and Protestant attitudes to divorce 71; and Protestant attitudes to women 71; and Protestant political affiliation 73; and Protestant denominations 77; and Protestant theological spectrum 97-99; and occuptional background 114-115; comparison of Catholic and Protestant churchgoers 144

Alliance Party 56, 58, 59-62, 73, 89, 109-110. See also political party

Baptist. See Protestant denominations

bi-confessionalism 3

Bible: reading and Catholics 18-20; Catholic beliefs about 23; reading and Protestants 69, 100, 128; Protestant beliefs about 78, 95, 99, 128-129; comparison of Catholic and Protestant practices 147

Blacks 45-50, 72, 87, 122

Boal, F.W. 95

Bogardus Social Distance Scale 45

Breslin, A. 24, 26

Brethren. See denominations

Campbell, J.A. 95

capital punishment 39, 106, 109, 130-131; comparison of Catholic and Protestant attitudes 152-153

Catholic church: as one true church 27; as institution 32-35;

Catholic churchgoers 7-67 *passim*; and age 7, 21-22; and gender 7; and occupational background 7; and education 7, 22-23; and unemployment 7; and modernisation, 8, 9; and secularisation, 8, 9; and ecumenism, 8; and liturgical reform, 8; and sacraments, 8; and religious practices 10-20; and conflict in Northern Ireland 9; sacramental participation of 10-20; and mass attendance 10-16; and attendance at confession 11-16; and devotional piety 16-20; and Church teachings 20-32; and

patterns of belief 20-24; and belief levels 24-27; and orthodoxy 24-27; and role of individual conscience 27-29; and guidance 28-29; and importance of religion 29-32; and upbringing of children 30-31; and mixed marriage 31; and traditionalism 31; moral and social concerns of 32-43; and attitudes to lay participation 32-33; and attitudes to the role of women in the church 33-34; and relevance of liturgy 34-35; and impact of social change 35-43; and private morality 35-39; and contraception 36-37; and attitudes to abortion 37-38; and attitudes to divorce 38-39; and discipline in society 39-42; and attitudes to gender roles 42-43; and religious mixing 44-45; and social mixing 45-55; and attitudes to mixing in schools 53-55; and identity 55-62; and political outlook 55, 62-66; and experience of the Troubles 60-61; and constitutional aspirations 64-65; and perceptions about equality 61, 65-66; and social solidarity 62, 66-67; compared with Protestant churchgoers 143-170 *passim*
Catholic exclusivity 52-53
Catholic schools 30-31, 53-54; and national identity 58
Chinese 45-50, 72, 87, 122
Church of Ireland. See Protestant denominations
church sites 4-5
churchgoing as symbolism 4-5
clergy: interviews 5
community relations 44-55, 72, 84-88, 102-106, 117-118, 118-123, 133-138; comparison of Catholic and Protestant attitudes 159-163. See also ecumenism
community: Protestant and Catholic, 1, 2; sense of among Catholic and Protestant churchgoers 147, 156
commuting 147-148
confession 26
confession attendance 11-16; influence of age 12-14; influence of education 14-15; influence of occupational background on 15; influence of employment status 15; influence of gender 15-16
conflict: in Northern Ireland 3, 9
Congregrational. See Protestant denominations
conservative. See theological spectrum
constitutional future 64-65, 72-73, 110-111; comparison of Catholic and Protestant attitudes 167-168
contraception: Catholic attitudes to 36-37
conversion 69, 79, 95, 111-112, 128-129; comparison of Catholics and Protestants on 147

De Gregory, J.L. 3, 63
denominational clusters 74-77
denominations. See Protestant denominations
devil 26, 69, 99
devotional piety: see Bible reading, prayer, sacramentals, sacraments
discipline in society: Catholic attitudes to 39-42, 61-62; and age 40; and education level 40-41; Protestant attitudes to 106, 130-131; comparison of Catholic and Protestant attitudes 152-153
divorce: Catholic attitudes to 38-39; Protestant attitudes to 71, 106-107, 109; comparison of Catholic and Protestant attitudes 150-151
Dunlop. J. 153
DUP 73, 88-89, 109-110, 125, 134-135. See also political party

ecumenism 8, 44-45, 81-84, 102-104, 117-118, 133-134; comparison of Catholic and Protestant attitudes to 157-159. See also community relations
education: and Catholics 7, 53-55; influence on attendance at Mass 14-15; influence on attendance at confession 14-15; and Bible reading 18-19; and patterns of Catholic belief 22-23; and Catholic orthodoxy 25-26; and importance of religion to Catholics 29; and attitudes to discipline in society 40-41; and religious mixing 44; and attitudes to mixed marriage 51-52; and Protestant denominations 77; and theological spectrum 98; and political party 127
employment status: influence on attendance at Mass 15; influence on attendance at confession, 15; and Catholic beliefs about guidance 29
English 45-50, 87
ethnicity 1, 4
Evangelical Presbyterian. See Protestant denominations
evangelical. See theological spectrum

fairness, sense of 61, 65-66, 88, 122, 137-138; comparison of Catholic and Protestant attitudes 166
female altar servers 33
Free Presbyterian. See Protestant denominations
fundamentalist. See theological spectrum

Galliher, J.F. 3, 63
gender: and Catholic churchgoers 7; influence on attendance at Mass 15-16; influence on attendance at confession, 15-16; and sacramentals, 17; and

language in liturgy 34-35; Catholic attitudes to 42-43; and Protestants churchgoers 68; and occupational background 114-115, 117; comparison of Catholic and Protestant churchgoers 143-144, 148-150. See also women
gendered language 34-35, 80, 100, 130; comparison of Catholic and Protestant attitudes 149

heaven 26, 99
hell 26, 99

identity: and Catholics 55-62; and Protestants 110-111; 123-127; comparison of Catholic and Protestant attitudes 163-166
Independent Evangelical Church. See Protestant denominations
Indians 45-50, 72
individual conscience 27-29
individualism: and Catholic piety 19-20; and Protestant denominations 81

Keane, M.C. 9

laity: Catholic attitudes 32-33
language: power of 171-172. See also gendered language
Lewis, C.S. 4
Ley, D. 1
liberal. See theological spectrum
life after death 26
liturgy: Catholics and reform of 8; relevance of to Catholics 34-35
Livingstone, D.N. 95
Loughran, G. 53
Lyons, F.S.L. 2

McEwan, A. 98
MacIntyre, A. 142
McMackin, T. 53
marriage. See mixed marriage
Martin, D. 95
mass attendance 10-16, 27; influence of age 12-14; influence

of education 14-15; influence of occupational background 15; influence of employment status 15; influence of gender 15-16
Methodist. See Protestant denominations
methodology 174-183
mixed marriage 31, 45-47, 50-53, 87, 104-105, 122, 136-137; comparison of Catholic and Protestant attitudes to 159-160
modernisation: and Catholics 8, 9
Moffat, C. 53
monoliths 1-3, 4, 5-6, 62, 67, 112
morality scales 39, 91-92, 229
morality: and Catholics 32-43; sexual 35-39, 108-109, 150; private 35-39, 130-131; public 39-43, 132-133; and Protestants 70-72, 91-94, 106-109; comparison of Catholic and Protestant attitudes 150-154
Moravian. See Protestant denominations
Murray, D. 22, 53

national identity: and Catholics 56-58; and Protestants 73, 110-111, 138-141; comparison of Catholic and Protestant attitudes 163-164
neighbourhood 4, 44, 87-88, 105, 118-121, 135-136, 147-148; comparison of Catholic and Protestant perceptions 154-157, 160, 162-163
neighbours 46-47, 48-50
Nic Ghiolla Phádraig, M. 24
Non-Denominational Fellowship. See Protestant denominations
Non-Subscribing Presbyterian. See Protestant denominations
Northern Ireland: naming 55-56; political future of 58

O'Brien, C.C. 3
occupational background: and Catholic churchgoers 7; influence on attendance at Mass 15; influence on attendance at Confession 15; and Protestant churchgoers 68, 77, 112-127; and theological spectrum 98, 114; and denomination 113-114; and political party 127; comparison of Catholic and Protestant churchgoers 145
O'Connor, F. 63
Orange Order 110, 125, 126, 138, 139-140
ordination of women 33-34, 80, 100-101, 129, 148-149
Orientalism 1, 2
orthodoxy of Catholics: and levels of belief 24-27; and age 25; and education 25-26; and importance of religion 29
orthodoxy scale 24
O'Sullivan, O. 32

papal infallibility 23, 27, 32
Pentecostal. See Protestant denominations
Philadelphia 1
place identity: and Catholics 55-56, 60; and Protestants 123; comparison of Catholic and Protestant sense of 164-165
political identity: and Catholic churchgoers 58-62; and Protestant churchgoers 88-91, 123-127. See also politics
political party: and national identity 58, 138-141; and Catholic affiliation 58-62; and Protestant affiliation 72-73, 109-112, 124-125, 127-141; comparison of Catholic and Protestant preferences 165-166
politics: 62-66. See also political identity, political party
population balance 139, 168
prayer: and Catholic churchgoers 17-18; and Protestant churchgoers 100, 128; comparison of Catholic and Protestant churchgoers 146-147

Presbyterian. See Protestant denominations
Protestant churchgoers 68-142 *passim*; and age 68, 97-98; and gender 68; and occupational background 68, 112-127; religious beliefs of 69-70, 77-84, 99-100; and moral attitudes 70-72, 91-94, 106-109, 130-131; and cross-community interaction 72, 84-88, 102-106, 133-138; and political attitudes 72, 88-91, 109-112, 123-127, 127-141; and national identity 73, 110-111, 138-141; denominational features 74-94; and interdominational migration 78-79; and church attendance 79, 99-100, 116-117; and ordination of women 80, 100-101; and gendered language 80, 100; and individualism 81; and inter-church relations 81-84, 102-104, 133-134; and attitudes to mixing in school 85-86, 104-105, 121-122, 136-137; and mixed marriage 87, 104-105, 122, 136-137; and neighbourhood composition 87-88, 105, 118-121, 135-136; and perceptions about equality 88, 122, 137-138; and attitudes to United Ireland 89-90, 110-111; and sense of community cohesion 90-91, 125-126; and geographical space 91, 140; and the theological spectrum 94-112; and religious and class solidarity 136; and population balance 139; compared with Catholic churchgoers 143-170 *passim*
Protestant denominations 74-94; and interdominational migration 78-79; and doctrinal orthodoxy 78-79; and church attendance 79; and women's ordination 80; and gendered language 80; and individualism 81; and inter-church relations 81-84; and cross-community relations 84-88; and attitudes to mixing in school 85-86; and mixed marriage 87; and neighbourhood composition 87-88; and perceptions about equality 88; and political identity 88-91; and sense of community cohesion 90-91; and geographical space 91; and private morality 91-92; and public morality 93-94; and theological spectrum 96-97; and occupational background 113-114

questionnaire: design 175-176; distribution and collection 176-177; response to 177-179

racial monolith 1
religion: significance of 3-5
religious practices: among Catholics 10-20; among Protestants 69, 116-118; comparison of Catholic and Protestant churchgoers 146-148
resurrection 26, 69, 78, 99
Robinson, E. 98
rosary. See prayer
Rose, R. 3, 63

sacramentals 16-17
sacraments: and Catholics 8, 10-20, 27
Said, E. 1-2
sample: size determination 175; reliability 180-182; weighting of response 182-183
schools 53-55, 85-86, 104-105, 121-122, 136-137; comparison of Catholic and Protestant attitudes 160-161
SDLP 58, 59-62, 65. See also political party
Second Vatican Council, *see* Vatican II
secularisation: and Catholics 8, 9
security situation 166

sin 23, 26
Sinn Fein 58, 59-62. See also political party
social change: impact on Catholics 35-43; impact on Protestant attitudes 71-72
social class. See occupational background
social concerns: of Catholics 32-43
social mixing 45-55, 72, 84-88, 102-106, 133-138
Southern Irish 45-50, 87
spaces: religious 4-5
speaking in tongues 69, 78, 99
stereotyping 1-3, 4, 5-6, 168-170, 171-172
Sunday observance 70, 101-102, 131; comparison of Catholic and Protestant attitudes 153-154
survey: selection of areas 174; selection of churches 174-175; sample size determination 175; questionnaire design 175-176; questionnaire distribution and collection 176-177; response 177-179

territory 62, 125; comparison of Catholic and Protestant attitudes 168
theological spectrum 94-112; and denomination 96-97; and demographic characteristics 97-99; and educational attainment 98; and religious convictions 99-100; and religious practice 99-100; and gender 100-101; and Sunday observance 101-102; and community relations 102-106; and moral attitudes 106-109; and political persuasion 109-112;

and occupational background 114
Todd, J. 63
transubstantiation 27
Troubles, The: Catholic experience of 60-61; caused by politics or religion 62-64, 125; comparison of Catholic and Protestant experience 155-156
two traditions, 2, 143, 168, 171-172
typecasting 1-3

unemployment: among Catholics 7; comparison of Catholic and Protestant churchgoers 145-146
Unionist Party 73, 88, 109-110, 125. See also political party
United Ireland: Catholic views about 64-65; Protestant views about 89-90, 110-111, 123-124, 125, 139

Vatican II 8, 19-20, 32, 35, 43
Virgin Mary 27

Wallis, R. *et al*, 63
Weafer, J. 24, 26
West, the 1
Whelan, C. 31
Whyte, J. 63
Wittgenstein, L. 171
women: Catholic attitudes to role of 33-34; Catholic attitudes to ordination of 33-34; Protestant attitudes to role of 69-70, 71, 117, 130; Protestant attitudes to ordination of 80, 100-101, 129; comparison of Catholic and Protestant attitudes to 148-150
work: social mixing at 46, 47-48, 162